Dr Louise Mahler

RESONATE

For people who need to be heard

VIKING
an imprint of
PENGUIN BOOKS

ABOUT THE AUTHOR

Louise is a proven performer in leading individuals and groups to improve their presence and influence, through her unique perspective focusing on the trinity of mind, body and voice.

With a background in opera as well as a strong business background (PhD, Bachelor of Economics, Master of Applied Management in Service Management and Innovation, Master Practitioner in Neuro Linguistic Programming), she has brought the worlds of art and business together in a pioneering combination that breaks the barriers of standard communication and begins the process of getting truly behind your mask.

Louise is an international speaker who also conducts workshops and online programs to embed the learning. She contributes regularly to *The Financial Review* and other media.

For more see louisemahler.com.au

PRAISE FOR **RESONATE**

'If you meet Louise you will never forget her – she certainly makes a strong impression. Louise has a powerful message which she delivers in a way that makes you sit up and take notice. I was delighted to work with her at a conference we hosted for managing partners from across the globe. I was even more delighted when, six months later, they were still raving about Louise.'

Peter Kennedy
Managing partner, Madgwicks

'Louise Mahler's insights are a rich synthesis of the power that comes from how we communicate, which is often more influential than what we actually say. Her observations are simple yet profound – her wisdom not only pertains to the art, but also to the science of communication and how each and every one of us can adopt practical techniques to turbo-charge our impact.'

Lisa Claes
Executive director, Customer Delivery, ING Direct

'If you do a lot of public speaking and only have time to read one book this year, make it Dr Louise Mahler's. I have learnt more in a couple of hours with Louise than in several previous courses on public speaking combined.'

Christine Nolan
CEO, Breast Cancer Network Australia

'Wow! I have seen Louise turn nervous, ugly ducklings into calm, cool, confident swans with real presence who can illuminate a room. The secrets in this essential book will do it for you too.'

Winston Marsh

National president, National Speakers Association of Australia

---

'Louise Mahler provides the most successful antidote for unconvincing, diffident, lacklustre presentations in an inspirational, witty, well-researched manner. Anyone who wants to make an impact and convince their audience – whether that's the boss, the board or their colleagues – must read this book.'

Hon. Fran Bailey

Former federal minister and current board chairperson

'Louise Mahler's career has been rich in diversity, energy and creative achievement, from Europe's leading opera stages to the fields of intense business competition. Louise has seen it all, and in *Resonate* she sets out a compelling picture as to how a life and career can be characterised from the potential inherent in our voices. In Louise we have a role model for the power and versatility of vocal intelligence. A life and career has many chapters. No matter how successful we might have been to date, there are always positive ways to re-engineer and enhance who we are and what we do, as *Resonate* explains. This is a life Louise has lived herself, and the authority of that experience shines through its pages. I am sure this book will, in fact, resonate with all who read it. It does with me, and will sit on my personal highly recommended list for many years to come.

Peter Wilson
AM FAHRI

'Dr Louise Mahler has done for "vocal intelligence" what Daniel Goleman did for EQ! She has made the well-tuned mind-body-voice cycle, once solely the domain of the stage performer, accessible to the corporate communicator. Louise has energetically demonstrated time and again on our flagship executive program that "voice is a choice" and an vital antidote to communication failure. This pragmatic and quirky book is a necessary read for discerning executives and will be particularly helpful for those aspiring to global business positions.'

Clarence Da Gama Pinto
Senior consultant, Executive Education, Melbourne Business School
Senior Fellow, Leadership, Melbourne Business School

'My first impression of Louise Mahler was of a brilliant whirlwind of a woman and I am delighted to say that this is a brilliant whirlwind of a book. I spent a wonderful day working with Louise and knew immediately that I was in the company of a true teacher. Her skills and passion were palpable. More importantly, the clues and insights to finding your voice within these pages are so valid that they could change your life.'

Kerry Armstrong
Actor, author, teacher and director

'Everyone can learn something new from Louise, from the beginner at public speaking to the accomplished professional who does it every day for a living. Because she has found a new and fresh bag of tricks we all enjoy trying out – again and again – to become sharper, more convincing and inspiring. To let our true self and potential to surface. Suddenly the horrors of being on show become fun. Go on – try a few and then you'll want more.'

Andrew MacKenzie
CEO of BHP

'The only thing better than Louise's tremendous experience and knowledge in artful, impactful and engaging communication is her extraordinary ability to translate this into meaningful tools for mere mortals. She gives you the courage and confidence to find your voice and your body. And the results are nothing short of amazing. It's one thing to know your stuff, but quite another to be able to persuade, influence and entertain. In *Resonate*, the art of knowing your mind, body and voice comes together to create effective, lively communication – your audience will be delighted and you will feel utterly fantastic.'

Dr. Liz Walker
CEO, RSPCA Victoria

———

'*Resonate* is a contemporary, incisive communication bible for politicians, businesspeople, teachers and influencers. In this day and age leaders are scrutinised for the way they present as much as they are for the substance of their message. *Resonate* reinvigorates interest in the art of communication.'

Christine Fyffe
MP State Member for Evelyn

———

'Breath giving! This book provides keys to unlock uncertainty and doubt, allowing you to voice your authentic self with impact and persuasion. Louise's writing is clear, honest, witty and kind and I know everyone who reads it will learn and grow. I'm going to create a list from this book and hang it in my office where I will see it every day, reminding me to practise, practise, practise.'

Cassandra Michie
Partner, Pricewaterhouse Coopers

———

'Classical ballet dancers spend their lives working to make their art seem easy. Good public speakers work just as hard to make it seem as if it is no effort at all.

'Dr Louise Mahler teaches that hard work rather than natural talent will make you a fabulous speaker and presenter. I've watched people change for the better after working with Louise, as she reveals what the mirror can't. It is a wonderful transformation to watch, and I have been confronted myself. Come along with Louise for the ride: it will be hard and sometimes embarrassing work, but it will be worth it in the end. Trust me.'

Merita Tabain
Director, Media and Corporate Communications Department, Victoria Police

———

'This book is full of practical ideas to help you connect your body and voice; it will create self-awareness and enable you to truly resonate with your audience. You will also find yourself understanding others better. You can hear Louise's voice in this book: her relatable stories, her practical advice and her humour all shine through. *Resonate* is simply a must-read for anyone whose key role is communication – it will leave you singing.'

Sadhana Smiles
CEO, Harcourts Group Victoria Pty Ltd

———

'If you have ever feared that people walk out of your presentations saying they wished it was time they could get back, read this book. Louise Mahler is a diva in the true sense of the word: self-assured, confident and a grand performer. As you read, you will feel her presence filling the room. Louise's joyful, self-deprecating approach will give you the confidence to embrace your true voice and her practical, down-to-earth tips will guide you through conquering common blocks to help you engage your audience.'

Catherine Ordway
Professor of Practice, La Trobe University

———

'This book is essential for anyone who wants to express themselves confidently and clearly. *Resonate* leaves you inspired and empowered, with new tools and techniques to assert yourself clearly and confidently, enabling effective self-expression in any environment. Louise is an expert in both delivering powerful and inspiring talks all over the globe and training others to do the same, working with people at all levels, from politicians and large corporations to small business owners. Once you read this book and become aware of how connected self-expression is to voice, as well as discovering easy tools to improve your communication, it is hard not to feel more confident, whether you're onstage speaking to a large audience, or in a small group of friends.'

'*Resonate* delivers a very important message which everyone can benefit from: how to embrace your voice and learn to communicate effectively, clearly and confidently. The powerful tools that Louise shares come from her years of experience as an opera singer, international keynote speaker and vocal trainer. The tips found in this book will be extremely valuable to anyone who wants to express themselves well, influence people's thinking, or clearly argue an opinion. *Resonate* has made me aware of simple things I can improve in my communication, which has made me feel instantly more confident and self-aware.'

Steph Woollard
Founder, Seven Women, and winner of the 2014 Ethical Enterprise Award

———

'To sing is an expression of your being,
a being which is becoming.'

Maria Callas

CONTENTS

FOREWORD

I congratulate Louise on this delightful, inspirational book, which will be useful to everybody, including health professionals, corporate workers and the public. Louise has drawn on her incredible life experience to write this erudite work, from her early childhood experiences to her current incarnation as a successful professional, corporate communicator and highly sought-after international public speaker.

When you meet Louise she displays passion, humour, authenticity, compassion, charm, flair and honesty – qualities that are on display in abundance in this book. Louise is honest and tells it as it is, with humility, integrity and honesty. Her resilience and ability to change and transform her life have inspired many people, and her story will give hope to many who have experienced failures in their lives too. She is right: we have all had some negative experience with expressing our feelings through voice. *Resonate* takes us on a journey of transformation, and will show you how to be aware of and reflect on how you speak and express yourself. It does more, too: it will help you to reclaim your voice and lift your blockages to reveal your true potential. You'll learn to express yourself through voice in a way that is joyful and fun, recognise the mind-body-voice connection, and allow the natural voice to express who you truly are. Louise shows you how to be heard, be felt, take control and communicate effectively.

Mind-body medicine is fundamental to holistic healing, and this is an area of growing interest for my profession, medicine. Louise is a pioneer in her field; she has worked with patients experiencing disability and terminal illness, and her strategies may one day be part of routine treatment for patients suffering chronic diseases. From my perspective as a health professional who works closely with patients, Louise offers a safe therapeutic tool for healing as part of their overall management plan. The potential is enormous for training health workers and anyone who wants to help patients. Beyond this, her strategies can be used in every workplace in training staff. I believe her work could actually change the world.

I am extremely proud of Louise and I am sure you too will love this book.

Associate Professor Dr Vicki Kotsirilos
MBBS, FRACGP, FACNEM
Medical Practitioner and Professor of Nutrition

PART ONE

Getting started

INTRODUCTION

---

*Voice is a choice! Your choice about
the person you present to the world.*

Go to any airport – Tokyo, New York, Berlin, St Petersburg,
Sydney – and you will hear a different sound, a different tone,
in the chatter going on around you. Every culture has its own
vocal sound. The Germans are low in pitch and crisp on their
air flow at the end of sentences. A lot of Australians speak
with a twang. And on top of our cultural differences, we all
have our own individual twist on voicing. Some of us sound
as if we have a football down our throats, some sound as if
a rope is tied around our necks and quite frankly some just
sound like pillocks (yes, that's a technical term).

Yet all babies are born able to make the same sounds.
Not only that but – as any sleep-deprived parent will confirm –
babies know how to communicate very clearly and forcefully to
let you know they need something, even though they can't yet
speak. When we're babies, the singing, gurgling, free-wheeling

expression of self is as natural as breathing. By the time we reach adulthood, half of us can't even hum a tune! So what went wrong?

Our ability to communicate is innate, but the very experience of growing up buffets our natural mind-body-voice cycle in a powerful continuum that I call 'vocal intelligence'. When your vocal intelligence is compromised or even destroyed, so is your ability to communicate effectively. You lose your presence and influence because, whether you like it or not: *You are your voice and your voice is you.*

It's the unthinking criticism we copped as a child, the embarrassment we suffered in adolescence, the snide aside shot at our adult self – all of these and other stresses of the modern world pile on, strangling our natural voice and muddling our sound.

This confidence-pounding happens to us all to varying degrees, even the most outwardly assured. The paradox is that, because we can't *see* our voices, or feel what happens in the larynx, we don't even hear our own voices as others do. We live in blind ignorance of our capacity to voice and often don't even realise when we've let it slip away and lost its majesty, even though (and I'll keep saying it), you are your voice and your voice is *you.*

I'm here to tell you that voice is a choice. You can reclaim, restore and revitalise your vocal intelligence, and I'm going to show you how.

And it's not about 'faking it to make it'; it's about authenticity, credibility and clarity: knowing yourself and being heard – getting your message across and even feeling great while doing it!

Whether you're struggling to make your point in a work meeting or a P&C gathering, whether you're going for the next big job or trying to improve your performance in the one you already have, and even if you just want better ways to communicate with your friends and the people you love, this book will show you how to tune in to your own vocal psyche, identify the physical and mental blocks that are holding you back, and take back ownership of your authentic voice.

Let me make something clear. This is not the normal business approach of researching the way others see us and then pandering to their needs. This is about understanding who you are and your patterns of engagement, and taking control. Even if you're a confident public speaker, I'll give you tools to use in sticky situations, and we'll tune up your instrument and show you how to play it. And if speaking in public, even in a small meeting, is your idea of purgatory, I will show you the way out.

How did I come to be doing this? I've trained all my life as a performer – I love to sing. But, don't worry: I'm not going to ask you to sing. Well, maybe a little hum won't hurt.

It's all just a little bit of history repeating

My adventures in voice began at home. Ours was hardly the Bach family, with generations of excellence in music, but we knew how to voice. I was born and raised in Brisvegas and music filled our family home (what else did you do in the dormitory suburbs of Dizzy Brizzy?). And I was always in full voice singing hymns at school assemblies (I was certainly never one of the girls Sister Anne had to encourage to join in).

At home, there was inevitably some form of song blaring from the record player. I remember Connie Francis and Shirley Bassey, *Chu Chin Chow* and *Pagliacci* – nothing shy or retiring – and the whole family sang along, generous with the volume. Singing for me was already a passion. But let's not play the happy family card. I had an absent father, a chronically depressed mother and a sister who loathed the fact of my existence (but more of that in my next book, *Advanced Attention Seeking as a Form of Self Defence in the Dysfunctional Family*). You might say that music and laughter are important ingredients in joyful times, but they also served to express a broader range of emotions such as sadness, frustration and loss. One of my favourites, 'How can I sing from a heart that's cold?' from *Chu Chin Chow*, is hardly a merry-go-round of bliss.

My father had one of those voices that truly boomed – it was a deep roar, the kind of voice that when you hear it, you do a double take: 'What was that?!' It was extraordinary. He died when I was young, and that had a major impact on me, partly because he was a hugely credible, dominant presence thanks to that enormous voice. My father worked so hard that I didn't really know him, but I sure knew his voice. When he died, the first thing I thought was, 'No! We don't have a recording of him!' That's the first thing I thought – because his voice was *him*.

My mother loved to sing – she had always wanted to be a singer, so she sang *all* the time. She told me that when she was very young she would sing with the Salvos on the main street in Wallumbilla in Central Queensland. As a homemaker, she sang in the morning, during the day and when night fell. And then she used to sing us to sleep! When she was the officer of the mess for the air force in Townsville, she used to stand on the table and sing for the troops. I grew up hearing stories from her about those times, standing on the table, singing. She thought she was a star – and she was very beautiful. Many years later, when she was in her eighties, she went to a WAAF reunion. One of the women said to her, 'I remember you, Carmel. You were that one who always made a fool of yourself.' And my mother never sang another note – never sang again. It was heartbreaking. (When she died, the first thing I thought was 'Yes, we *do* have a recording of her.')

And this is at the core of my work on vocal intelligence. The voice *is* heartbreaking. We're often happy to play the fool and have fun made of us in other ways. But when people criticise your voice, it's crushing. And that's because your voice is such a direct connection to who you are. Your voice is *who you are*, and we all know that intrinsically. And yet, again, because we can't see or feel the voice, its importance in relation to our psyches has largely been overlooked, which is crazy.

So when you criticise my singing – perhaps because it's my most authentic, vulnerable, deep expression of self – my heart is broken. And that extends, of course, to my speaking voice. You mock my voice, and that stays with me and blocks me. It doesn't matter whether I'm eight years old and my class speech has been mocked by my mates, or I'm eighty and my old WAAF colleague has just lobbed a bitter grenade at me. When you pour scorn on my voice, I shrivel up.

This book gives you the tools to identify and smash through the blockages that are boxing in your vocal intelligence – I call these blockages 'veils', so perhaps a better metaphor is to 'shred the veils'. And we're going to rip them down for good!

Let's start at the very beginning

I started doing singing lessons when I was sixteen, mainly because my mother wanted me to. It was a *very* unusual thing for a teenager to do at that time in Brisbane, and certainly none of my friends were doing it. But off I'd go to the Conservatorium on the train after school one day a week for my lessons, and I won a couple of leads in school plays and that was fun. So when I started at university I joined the Queensland Light Opera Company and we did *The Student Prince*. I was only in the chorus, but I remember standing on the table at the front, on the stage at Her Majesty's Theatre, and thinking, 'Oh, this is so *good*. This is great fun!' Just like my mother told me. I'd been bitten by the performing bug.

In spite of that early passion for singing, and the lessons, I played to my academic strength after high school and headed for an economics degree. I'm very good at maths (which often goes with musical ability), so I was doing all the statistics subjects and econometrics.

I got to the end of second-year statistics and thought, 'This is breathtaking – in all the wrong ways.' Meanwhile, my singing teacher said to me, 'You know, Louise, you should sing professionally.' So I started weighing it up: 'Let me see: Bureau of Statistics, or life upon the wicked stage? Life upon the wicked stage, or Bureau of Statistics?' I did finish my economics degree, but then I went straight to the Queensland Conservatorium.

When I look back on those years at the Conservatorium, I realise I had a spoilt, narcissistic existence. I'd go off to a singing teacher for a lesson focussed on me, me, *me*. Then

I'd have a piano lesson . . . which for me was a game of looking as if you can play the piano, when you really can't! And then there'd be a rehearsal session for a performance, followed by a dance lesson. It was just fun, fun, fun, fun. I got lots of the lead roles and I *loved* every minute of it.

During those years of study and practice (I ended up completing a music degree in both performance and teaching, a postgraduate diploma in opera and a licentiate of music), I also discovered the absolutely intoxicating experience of singing well. When it happened, it was as though someone else was singing through me; almost as if I had absolutely nothing to do with the sound I was producing, but had somehow lent my body to an invisible force that was controlling my every muscle. I felt I could do anything. (I have since learned this is a common sensation for singers.)

I started entering singing competitions and winning prizes and grants, and got it into my head that I wanted to take Europe. To fund the trip, I had saved some of my earnings from waitressing and raised money through concerts, and a friend of my mother's kindly gave me some money too.

The next few years were a whirlwind. I worked all over Europe with some of the heavyweights of the classical music world – Sir Peter Pears, Murray Perahia, Dame Elisabeth Schwarzkopf and Lucia Popp, to name just a few. Some of my most formative years were spent as part of the Vienna State Opera.

But despite the truly wonderful experience of being a part of the opera company, once Elisabeth Schwarzkopf had retreated from her teaching for personal reasons, I felt very alone in Vienna. And then the extreme winter began to get to me. We're talking -30°C, for a girl from the sub-tropics. I developed chronic bronchitis that I just could not shake. My voice faltered, my singing began to deteriorate and I stumbled through my performances, impressing no-one – least of all myself. I felt like *La Bohème*'s Mimi, slowly coughing to my death.

By this time, I'd also married and had a young son, Oliver. But, unable to continue with my singing, I left first the opera company, then my husband and finally Europe, returning home to Australia from London with a small child, no money and my tail between my legs. After all that success, I felt like a failure – and I was still coughing.

If I can't do, I won't teach

My family and friends all suggested that I should teach. But I wanted a new identity, and after the pain of what I saw as my failure in Vienna, I needed to remove myself as far from the world of voice as I possibly could. I had great qualifications and enormous experience, but I did not want a bar of teaching singing.

So for step one of my reinvention, I joined Australia's biggest – and perhaps blokiest – company. Let's call it BHP (because that's what it was!). Armed with my economics degree, I didn't mention my singing career because I feared it would somehow undermine my credibility. I began working with the division of maintenance and was quickly promoted to running quality for the engineering division. This soon evolved into training roles, and I have BHP to thank for the training I've received in every aspect of business you could imagine.

But even before I'd consciously concede it to myself, the way I approached this work was strongly influenced by all I'd learned in my singing training.

My deep knowledge of how the mind, body and voice are interconnected had been a part of my life for all those years at the Conservatorium in Brisbane, and then in Essen, Aldeburgh, London and Vienna. Now, I was seeing it much more clearly, and it was rapidly becoming obvious to me that the well-tuned mind-body-voice cycle is as critical to the corporate communicator as to the stage performer. I watched well-meaning managers failing to communicate effectively, simply because they lacked that crucial vocal intelligence.

Where was the breathing mastery of Pavarotti? Where was Schwarzkopf's artful use of air? Where was the power of Domingo? Instead, important ideas regularly fell by the wayside because of communication failure.

I was now working as a trainer with many different organisations and, at a time when 'inspirational change management' was the order of the day, leaders at all levels, in every organisation I saw, were expressing themselves abysmally. Presentations largely took the form of information 'dumps', with the only defining characteristics being aggressive confrontation or stifling monotonality. Even in one-on-ones, their voices were dry and emotionless. Physically, there was a lot of hunching over, shifting eyes, folded arms. And not just where I was – from multinationals to corner shops, there was, and still is, a pervasive lack of vocal intelligence.

In my training sessions – on subjects such as customer service, supervisor skills and team building – I slowly began sharing some of my performance-based ideas with my 'students'. I was still smarting after my tail-between-legs exit from Europe, but the closed doors of the training rooms afforded me some safety to begin reopening myself – and introducing my unwitting participants – to the joy of voice. They seemed to enjoy it too, so that encouraged me further. What's more, I could see that it was making a difference to their communications skills.

Buoyed by this, and ever-fascinated by learning, I began studying other areas to extend my knowledge in the mind-body-voice sphere. The more I learned, the more my ideas gathered steam for encouraging (and, let's face it, *fixing*) the voice at work. Voice is a choice and experience has taught me that everything is changeable. You just have to want to do it.

Even though I'd kept my 'life on the wicked stage' identity hidden at work, I was given to little bursts of song (I still am). One day, I was singing loudly to myself in the stairwell and emerged into the foyer of the organisation to find a receptionist staring at me. 'Was that you singing just then?' she asked. I hadn't realised that anyone could hear me through the fire doors, but I smiled shyly, and said yes. 'Don't give up your day job!' she cackled. I was wounded. She'd attacked my voice; without meaning to, she had attacked my very core. I'd had enough of this nonsense.

Soon enough, I would find a way to do just that: give up my day job to spread the word on vocal intelligence.

VOCAL INTELLIGENCE

Why we all need to tune up

I came up with the term 'vocal intelligence' because this whole process is about so much more than simply speaking. It's about analysing your mind-body-voice cycle, and then getting it into sync so it's running like a perfectly tuned Rolls-Royce engine. It's about understanding voice as a physical force and how we use it – and abuse it. And it's about unblocking yourself to set free the boundless power of your authentic voice.

When I began this journey, I was wearing my corporate hat, trying very hard to conform to the business world, especially as I'd just left behind the surreal existence of professional opera. But before I quite knew it myself, I was wielding my secret weapon, bestowed upon me during my past: powerful communication. And I mean powerful. On the stage, we could move people to tears. As a singer, I was a 'lyric dramatic' soprano – a style of voice that literally makes people cry.

Everyone's voice has a different impact. There are many different types of sopranos. There's dramatic soprano,

13

which makes you feel like, 'I'll kill him myself'. Then there's lyric, which makes you feel beautiful. And then there's lyric dramatic, which just makes you cry.

These different qualities of the voice come from the way it resonates – the vibrations caused by the action of our vocal folds (more on that later), and then through the resonance of air in the throat and mouth and then actually through the skin of whoever is hearing the voice. In fact, when we're hearing the voice, we're *feeling* it. The voice is physical (more on that later, too). Most people don't recognise it or think about it, but believe me when I tell you that it really helps so much to know what kind of voice you have, not in the sense of what flavour of opera singer you are, but in understanding the effect your voice has on people when you use it correctly. And that's a key part of vocal intelligence.

As I made my way up the corporate ladder, trying very hard to fit into the greyness, the importance of what I'd learned about voice during my performing years stayed with me. It became clear to me that the power of voice would come to imbue every facet of my life, even as I turned my back on the 'wicked stage'.

I gave in, and decided that the stage clearly had lots to offer to the corporate world. I decided to pursue further studies (I like to learn), and I began with a broad, voice-agnostic focus to connect business and the arts, beginning a Masters of Applied Science in Service and Innovation Management at RMIT University in Melbourne. I had some clever and supportive psychology professors at RMIT, and they pushed me towards focusing my study on the voice, rather than the arts as a whole. I was offered a full scholarship to do my PhD in

Business, with that focus. It seemed like self-destruction to me: *Who does voice?* I thought; no-one's talking about voice for voice's sake! There was precious little research in business – certainly, hardly any recent research – and no corporate market interested in pursuing voice training for their teams. And that was my professors' point.

Once I gave in to it, I realised that, armed with the vocal tools we singers learned to communicate vividly to big audiences in opera theatres, I had the makings of a magic formula. I could help people brighten up their workaday lives and – more importantly for many readers – improve business outcomes at the same time.

I've never been able to shake that part of me that is all about fun, fun, fun. In the first place, when I was working within the big corporation (years before I embarked on the academic side of my quest), I simply wanted to spare the world the all-too-common dull, airless death by workplace presentation. You've been in them. If you're honest, you've very likely *delivered* one. When your audience is sitting there daydreaming about how much more fun it would have been to read this presentation *while lying on a bed of nails*, you've not only failed in your communication, you've also compromised, corrupted and confused your message.

Getting a grip on your vocal intelligence will change all of that – for you and for the people for whom a root-canal session at the dentist would have been preferable to listening to you. Imagine having people look forward to one of your presentations! Envisage the day when you'll have to book a bigger room to accommodate your eager audience. Not only that, you'll enjoy it and love yourself doing it. That's what this is all about.

Vocal intelligence is crucial for all face-to-face communication, not just for those of you who need to hone your skills in presenting, dealing with the media or addressing a big boardroom meeting. It truly is vital at every level of personal interaction – even talking to yourself. And though I just said 'face-to-face', it's right there with you when you're on the phone, too – or talking over Skype, Viber or whatever type of digital comms lately tickles your device.

Essentially, if you're in a situation where your voice is the medium for your message, you must have your vocal smarts humming. Vocal intelligence is your inner genie in navigating difficult conversations with your partner, your kids or your best friend. It's indispensable when you're coaching the under-tens soccer side. And it's priceless when you want to gracefully grab the attention of the barista who seems more focused on that blonde bombshell who waltzed into the cafe after you. Of course, vocal intelligence is also a vital element in customer service – on either end of the interaction. And here's a fun secret: it even works when you're talking to your dog or horse (cats, not so much: their selective deafness turns even the most brilliant vocal intelligence into white noise – you can't win them all).

Conventional 'wisdoms' about voice that drive me crazy

Here are the common myths around voice. There are plenty more, but over the years I've distilled it down to these three fallacies – the ones that really bug me.

1. Your voice is invisible – and therefore it doesn't matter.
2. You're stuck with the voice you have; you can't change it.
3. Not everyone can sing.

I want you to realise that, even though we can't see it, voice is *physical*. Voice is moving air. It's a physical force; its vibrations touch everything and everybody who hears it. When you withdraw air and reduce its power, it's a subliminal message: 'I don't want to touch you. I don't care about you.' Your voice reflects your mental attitude and it literally broadcasts that attitude, whatever situation you're in. So, enough about voice not mattering. It's not only who we are; it's also how we feel.

Now, as to this notion that you're stuck with your voice, whether it's a strangled little squeak that no-one can hear or an aggressive bark that makes people tune out. No, no and *no* – you're not stuck with it. As you'll discover through this book, a lifetime of stresses and postural habits, as well as physical and psychological patterns of compensation, have compromised your communication and corrupted your innate vocal intelligence. It is not about expanding your potential, it is about rediscovering the perfection you were born with. Now you know that *voice is a choice*, you can do something about fixing it. Stop thinking you're condemned to continue with your voice the way it is, even if it's failing you. Just recognise that it's up to you to fix it – and reading this book is the key to recovery.

Now, the singing thing. I realise that most people aren't show-offs – show-offs are a special breed. You might not *want* to sing, but you absolutely can (and in my view, you should!).

When I was doing my PhD, dutifully researching the mighty power of voice as per my professors' push (and before I'd begun calling it vocal intelligence), I worked with people who were gravely ill with cancer as well as others who, for whatever reason, needed to focus on regaining their health. While we did sing in the sessions, my whole focus was to help get their sound out. They were at a point in their lives where it had never been more difficult or more important for them to be heard, to get their message across to their loved ones, but also release themselves to themselves. To express.

I'd get everyone to lie on the floor and, in that position, completely supported by the floor, and not having to look at other people or even at themselves – so it felt very safe – I'd ask them to sing. Sing anything. Sing 'Baa Baa Black Sheep'. Sing without fear or self-consciousness and listen to how beautiful they sounded. And so they'd lie there, and they'd sing. I'd worked with actors and singers, and when you are working with actors, it is a forensic challenge to find that one little habit that will change their whole sound. When you are working with people who have barely even tried to change their sound before, it is child's play. Some of these people were hearing their voice for the first time in their lives – I mean really *hearing* themselves and the inherent beauty and strength in their own voices. It meant something, to be able to show strength at a time when they were weakened by their health challenges, but in a place where they could hear themselves without being embarrassed, because there was simply no place for holding back in their lives any more.

So don't tell me 'not everyone can sing'.

As I said, those wonderful people gave me so much inspiration for my PhD. It was very powerful. I'd go home and think about things that had come up in the sessions, and it would often lead me down a new path of research and reflection. It certainly reinforced my belief that the body, mind and voice are connected, and that integrating them is as much about healing as communication. Which brings us back in a neat pirouette to the magic of the mind-body-voice cycle.

It's useful to think about the mind-body-voice cycle by seeing it in those three parts. First, we need to understand what's happening in the mind, and work out what emotional strings are pulling us. Stress? Anxiety? Exhaustion? Something seemingly unconnected to work that's weighing you down mentally? Something upsetting that happened to you when you were a child?

It could be as small as a mortifying stage performance when you were in primary school – for me, it was my performance as a golliwog when I was about five years old. I cartwheeled on to the stage in my highly dubious costume – and everyone laughed. I thought they were laughing *at* me, and I froze.

Clearly, I got over it, but for more people than you'd imagine, these kinds of very early embarrassments leave deep trenches in their psyches – acute pain points around speaking in public that continually trip them up, without them even knowing it. We'll explore how you can work to identify and deal with these mind blockages in the next chapter. Trust me, once you know your devil inside, you can exorcise it!

Second, we'll look very closely at the bodily patterns that are blocking your voice. Sometimes tweaking just one key bad habit you've fallen into over the years can make a tremendous difference to your feelings and the way you communicate, both in terms of your actual voice and in the way your audience perceives your message.

Let the body sing!

The connection between body and voice was made clear to me when I literally received a body blow at the Vienna State Opera. It was delivered by Professor Ellen Müller-Preis, who'd been an Olympic champion fencer. After her fencing days were over, Ellen began studying breathing and movement in earnest, and that led her inexorably to the voice. She studied with Moshé Feldenkrais, inventor of the Feldenkrais Method, and with Frederick Matthias Alexander, the actor and voice teacher who developed the Alexander Technique to overcome his own breathing problems and hoarseness during performance and public speaking.

By the time I met Professor Müller-Preis, she was well established with the Vienna State Opera and also taught at other professional theatre companies in Austria. Her theory was deceptively simple: voice training must be integrated with body training to allow the body to breathe. Her premise: 'If you let the body breathe, then you let the body sing!'

Quite simply, Professor Müller-Preis changed my life. In the early days of working with her, she asked me about my sway back. I really thought it was none of her business. I was sitting on the ground, explaining that it was caused by a fall on the basketball court when I was in my teens, when suddenly she thrust her knee into my spine and commanded me to perform a breathing exercise using my lower-back muscles. I screamed with fear. 'I'm going to become a para-plegic here in Vienna!' was my internal cry (yes, I know – what a drama queen).

But not only did I not become a paraplegic, I learned things about posture and movement that became critical to my life as a whole. Professor Müller-Preis' theories became a vital part of the mind-body-voice cycle I researched for my PhD, and are integral to my own teaching today.

Later in the book we'll go in-depth on physical blockages to voice and how you can release them – without the assistance of a bony Austrian knee in your back!

Understanding the spiral of sound

To understand the mind-body-voice cycle, I'm going to explain how the state of both your mind and body are reflected in your vocal tone. Having your mind and body in tune equals your voice being on song! Once you embrace and acknowledge the mind-body-voice cycle, you are on the path.

What underpins my theories of vocal intelligence? And how did I develop the techniques that will help you regain your voice? As I mentioned, my psychology professors were keen for me to explore the history and science of voice. I wanted to know where it all went so wrong for us – how did we strangle our own voices? Why does everyone in the Western world think they can't sing? One clue is in our culture. Even today, other cultures have few hang-ups around voice and performance. Singing is a vital part of African, Indian and Chinese cultures.

It's the Europeans who stuffed it up and – surprise, surprise – it came about because of greed, a desire to create an exclusive class and the compulsion to shut others out. 'Devoicing' others as a way to hold on to power is part of our culture.

As I researched the history of classical singing, I could see that the rot set in back in 17th-century Italy and the *bel canto* era. Literally, *bel canto* means beautiful singing, and I'm all for that. (An aside: the classic put-down term for opera singing is *can belto*.)

As the operatic art form increased in popularity, and the orchestras and opera houses grew bigger, too, teachers began cultivating singers whose voices could rise to that occasion: voices that were louder, stronger and bigger. Nothing wrong with that, either.

Where the nonsense began was when the teachers started saying they wouldn't take people unless they could already sing beautifully. That's one of the fallacies around voice that makes me hopping mad: 'Not everyone can sing.' Suddenly, singing became a rarefied skill, and those deemed not to have a natural gift for it were shut out – even though, until then, everyone had been happily singing along together (as they continued to do in other cultures).

After years of studying the available literature on the *bel canto* era, which spanned the 200 years between 1720 and the beginning of World War I, I got a picture of how the singers and teachers duped pretty much the rest of Europe into this belief that only God-given talent – as opposed to hard work, constructive teaching and correcting bad habits – could get you on to the professional stage. The *bel canto* mob (yes, I do see them as a mafia) used this deity-bestowed talent model as a prerequisite for accepting pupils for lessons. Teachers were cautioned that a pupil must have 'a voice and a disposition, that he may not be obliged to give a strict account to God of the parent's money ill spent' (Tosi, 1987).

I couldn't trace the birth of the vocal audition directly to *bel canto*, at least not through the literature. But it's clear to me that somewhere in this era, auditions were introduced. And rather than adjust their teaching to meet the needs of each eager pupil, these lazy good-for-nothings raised the bar: anyone hoping for admission to the hallowed halls of singing first had to prove that they could already do it. Imagine if we said to kids: 'Kindergarten? No admission unless you can already read, write and add up.'

There's a lot of literature on how other natural gifts became a part of *bel canto* acceptance. Apparently you had to possess 'a pleasing appearance, adequate breathing capacity, no malformations of the face, mouth or body, and a good ear' (Callaghan, 2000). Raising the bar yet higher, graceful posture and expression, as well as a positive mental attitude, became essential to acceptance into a *bel canto* studio. This provokes the question: when so many qualities were prerequisites, what on earth were they teaching their students?

As you can tell, I feel pretty strongly about this; I believe the *bel canto* mobsters rode roughshod over the joy of singing for all of the Western world. Perhaps I should thank them. After all, their shut-out methodology, passed down over the centuries, which managed to strangle the voices of so many people, has created a thriving business for me.

And the truth is, I spent many years in the rarefied world of *bel canto* inheritance myself. When I came out of singing,

I could view the singing world differently. I could see how self-obsessed I'd been; I could see that not everybody saw singing as central to life. Then I went into the business world and for a while, I swallowed that whole, too. I lived as if the norms by which the corporate world was operating – with all of those deathly dull presentations, for example – was the only way. Now I'm outside both of those worlds, with insights gained from both, and together they form vocal intelligence – a powerful tool you can use to enhance many aspects of your life. So let's get going.

HOW TO GET YOUR SHARE OF VOICE

Audience, influence and attention –
you can have them all!

This section will help you understand the 'seven veils', which are the key physical elements that hide our vocal intelligence. The lessons that follow are the 'incubation' phase of your vocal transformation, which I'll also explain in this chapter.

You remember the body language rage? Where we all got into this game of reading other people's intentions and emotional state by studying their postures and gestures – no listening required? If you fold your arms, you're closed. If you move your eyes, you're hiding something. If you clench your jaw, you're aggressive. If your grin is too cheesy and the skin around your eyes isn't crinkling, it's not a genuine smile. Smooth your hair while speaking and you're probably lying.

Forests of trees have been felled (and, more recently, millions of pixels expelled) on the secrets of body language.

The investigation goes on into how we perceive each other. And while I agree that it provides us with some fascinating information, it is simply not a vehicle for change. Smoothing out your body language alone – and please imagine me spreading my arms wide to convey my honesty as I tell you this – is not going to get you your share of attention.

Don't get me wrong, it's a great life skill to be able to read people's physical messages, and it's very important to become aware of how people perceive your gestures in face-to-face communication. Of course it is! We'll do some intensive work on gestures later. And aligning your own posture and muscles is absolutely essential for engaging your mind with your own powerful body, to deliver your full-bodied voice.

Engagement is the other missing piece in the non-verbal studies paradigm. Speaking and listening are actively interlinked – it's a two-way engagement and when you're the one speaking, you have to recognise that; go for the richness of full communication. You don't just want to talk *at* people – 'Oh, phew! Glad that's over, I got it all out.' You want to engage them.

In customer service training, there's something known as the 'servuction model'. The idea is that customer service workers should remain constantly aware that the person they're serving is an integral part of the process. There is no separation of customer and service person. You become one. Well implemented, it really helps the customer feel listened to and valued, whether they're a hospital patient, someone shopping for shoes or some poor devil on the phone to a call centre.

Think about it this way: as air passes from your mouth, the chance is high (if you are facing them) some of it will actually enter the people around you. Likewise, their air is in you.

In the end, it is fascinating to think that with every breath, we are most likely inhaling a tiny fraction of the same air breathed by Jesus and Buddha and other great figures. Think about it! We are not separate.

For our purposes, the servuction model means you're *on*, bringing yourself wholly to the engagement; you are part of a oneness of breath moving between bodies. You're unhindered and unblocked. You're communicating in a way that resonates with the listener, and you're actively listening, too. In terms of vocal intelligence, you're really *humming*!

So let's get you the tools you need.

The Stairway to the Stars

First, you have to embrace the fact that you're going to need to change some things and maybe face some hard truths. There are external factors that might push you, such as the need to be heard or the fact that someone around you suggests you need help, but this is never enough. It's a bit like the old joke: how many psychiatrists does it take to change a lightbulb? Just one, but the lightbulb has to want to change. (I'm playing all week, folks!)

When I was working at BHP, Sheila Sheinberg, a terrific change consultant from the US, came to coach us, and I've adapted some of what I learned from her sessions for my own 'change model'. Do Google her and check out her website, the Center for Life Cycle Sciences (www.sheilasheinberg.com) – there are a lot of ideas there. I call my change model the Stairway to the Stars.

Here's my diagram:

Within this, the impetus for change is seen as the fire under all we do and the box it burns is our set of paradigms around what we can and can't do, as well as our beliefs around our own skills, talents and natural gifts. The star represents the new way we approach ourselves and the stairs are simply our commitment to practice. While you're climbing the stairs there are raindrops that may fall and stop you from what you are trying to achieve. These are not real barriers, but imagined ones. Knowing all of these elements is an essential part of your change plan.

Of course, this is just a pictorial way of representing the simple change plan of:

- Where are you?
- Where do you want to be?
- How will you get there?
- What is your impetus for change (internal and external)?
- What are your barriers to success?

Next is the order in which we attack the problem. I see this in three stages (this is developed from *Heuristic Research* by psychologist Clark Moustakas, which I used in my PhD):

- *Immersion*: This involves identifying your motivations, including the formative experiences that contributed to the voice you have today, what you want to change and why. It involves understanding each of your habitual patterns down to the smallest movement, in both unstressed and stressed situations.

- *Incubation*: These are the steps you'll take to change, and are tackled in depth in the coming chapters, where you'll learn alternative patterns for doing things. In my diagram they're the stairway, but see the rain coming down over the stairs? Those raindrops represent the difficulties you'll encounter.

- *Illumination*: This is where it all comes together – sooner than you think!

You'll be digging deep to learn about yourself, identify what needs to change and set about making that change. We will focus on how to get your share of voice but, as you'll see, doing so will also unlock a much broader suite of personal strengths.

Put simply, our vocal dynamics echo our psychodynamics. Your state of mind resonates through your voice, firstly because your mind shapes your body's response and gestures in line with feelings of fear, comfort, anxiety, trust, joy and so on; and subsequently, those physical postures shape your voice. It's easy to see how unlocking your body can unlock your vocal resonance. But unlocking your body can also promote a more peaceful mind, and finding your resonance can bring pure joy, or at the very least, soaring confidence to the psyche. So there can be no vocal change without mental change, and there can be no mental change without vocal change.

And you have to want to change! It's confronting, but the rewards are freedom of expression, confidence in communication and the power to influence.

Take back the reins

I'm taking some time to talk about the process of change, because the psychology behind voice is complex. Almost every part of what happens when we make sound is governed by both our rational and our emotional minds, so it's important to understand how they work together.

Think of a centaur, the creature from Greek mythology with the body of a mighty horse and the torso and head of a man. I use the centaur as a metaphor for the battle going on inside each of us, between the emotional mind – the mighty horse body – and the rational mind, which is the head. Our job here is to bring control of the voice back to the rational mind, understand it and only let the emotional mind run the show when we want it to.

We are governed by both the emotional and rational mind, but the faster and stronger part is the horse: emotion rules, whether we realise it or not. So the rational mind must be better educated and disciplined. Also, there's a difference between natural and habitual. It is natural for us to hold our breath when we're stressed – it's part of the well-known fight or flight reaction. Just when you need it most – giving a presentation or making an important phone call – your breath deserts you. So we must learn to override the strong, quite natural responses, develop our new habits or patterns, and practise, practise, practise.

When I'm nervous or stressed and I have performance anxiety, the horse part goes: quick, jam your diaphragm! Boom! Jam! It's automatic. On page 56 I explain how to kick it free: cough, do a breathing exercise – use your rational mind to put your emotional mind back in its box.

There's another thing that happens when we are asked a question we don't want to answer: we close our mouths. We clench. Another strong, fast response courtesy of our mighty, horse-driven mind. It's like a kneejerk of the jaw! So we have to teach our rational mind to lead the reactions, and instead to put into practice the physical response we need to unclench. One trick is to press your tongue and release the jaw – more about that on page 111.

31

So this is what I promise: we will learn to override our emotional responses and train the rational part of ourselves to lead. You cannot stop the emotional mind from having a reaction, but you can make a choice not to hold on to that reaction. The emotional mind directs natural physiological responses that are often unhelpful – certainly when we're dealing with performance anxiety.

So for the sake of your voice, you have to learn to stop letting that strong, fast emotional part of you lead your physical response. Think of it as the mindful part of vocal intelligence. It's 'think on your feet', not 'stomp on your thinking'. And if you practise, practise, practise, and embed all the new patterns so they are second nature, it will become easier and easier.

First, the immersion step

Where are you? Where do you want to be? What's stopping you getting there? What's the fire beneath you, inspiring you to make the change right now (basically, what made you pick up this book)?

Maybe you want to be heard in meetings at work, or to get a promotion, or to be able to speak to your teenage kids more effectively (let me know how that goes). Maybe someone's told you that your stilted or stunted communication skills are holding you back, professionally or personally. Maybe it's your own frustration at not being heard. For whatever reason, you've recognised that right now you're not getting your share of voice out there.

In my smaller workshops, I facilitate this immersion process personally for each participant, without them being aware that we're doing it. I don't lay it out for them as I'm doing for you now. We dive right in. I get every single person to speak. Soon after that, I usually get them to make a little impromptu talk. Please tell us why you're here and what you're going to talk to us about – pretend we're someone you're trying to present to right now. Make us care. Go!

I know it's hard – I watch people press back so hard against the backs of their chairs, I wonder if they're hoping a magic hatch will open up and evacuate them. But it's such a revealing, useful exercise and it serves up a lot of information about them. I watch them, identifying their vocal patterns, their physical habits, their posture, their eye movements, their learning preference, their source of power – everything. I listen to what they say, I try to figure out what they're thinking, and I watch those three things: mind-body-voice.

I study each person as they speak and, in just a few short exercises, I'll get it all. A lot of it is about the patterns – we fall into a bad one at some point and it becomes ingrained. Unless we've had a reason to hold a mirror to ourselves like this, we don't see these self-defeating habits but, trust me, everyone else does. They're often *really* obvious. And if they're obvious, they're distracting from the message you're trying to deliver, and however familiar your audience might be – even if they love you to bits – you've lost them.

The other day, I got a young woman up from among a large group. She works for a big charitable organisation and part of her job is to approach people and ask them to consider the charity during estate planning – to include the charity in their will. That's not an easy task: broaching the topics of death and money with a complete stranger. The organisation brought me in to help its staff improve their interactions with potential donors, and also to fine-tune their powers of persuasion.

So we were off and running in the workshop and I got this young woman up – in front of all of her colleagues, most of whom were older than her – and said, 'Could you greet the group, and just open your arms when you do it, please?' She said, 'Yes, I can.' Then she turned to the audience and said, 'Good. Morning. Everybody.' And as she did this, her hands moved in short chopping motions, in front of her body, almost in time to her words. I said, 'OK, well first of all, that gesture is a karate chop, I think we're looking more for a cuddle.' I demonstrated: arms outstretched, palms facing the audience, wide, welcoming.

It's natural that people become defensive at the start of these sessions, and she did. She said: 'I do ballet!' I replied, 'Yes, I can see that.' I stepped in and repositioned her arms. I moved them out, putting them into that expansive gesture with palms open. I stepped back and asked her to try again. Boom! She went straight back to karate chop.

I put my hand on her back and tried to straighten her up, as well as adjusting her hands again. By now, she was angry with me. She snapped, 'Well, I can't do it! I have a bad back.' (Echoes of my cries to Professor Müller-Preis as she thrust her knee in my spine.) From the get-go, her posture also meant that her voice was jammed up, too. I needed to show her that it would all be okay. And quickly!

Now, believe me, I am not talking about massive bodily manipulations here. I'm not asking the body to do anything unusual. It's more a matter of seeing where the body is doing something that it should not be doing.

So I gently got her standing correctly. She said, 'Well, I feel ridiculous.' By then she'd already partly snapped back into her habitual posture and I had to move her again, to get her standing tall and strong. I manipulated her into that position again and said, 'Okay. Are you still feeling ridiculous?' She said, 'Yes, I feel *absolutely stupid*.' I said, 'Well, here's where I tell you: that's only your perception. You think you look stupid, but let's ask the group. Hands up if you think that looks okay?' Every hand in the room goes up. 'Hands up if you thought the other position looked tense.' Again, the whole room.

This was exactly what she needed to hear many years earlier, but so much of this work is 'undiscussable'. The pain of making mistakes is too hard. We learn by trial and error and often come up with the wrong conclusions, but at least we are still alive. Making changes can feel very threatening to our psyches.

What was great, and where this lesson was so powerful, was that she went from being cranky to believing it. She took it on board, thought about how she was standing, greeted the room again retaining the correct position, and she was *great*. Her voice was stronger, and her gesture was in keeping with the greeting. She got it! What's more, everyone in the room could hear it. Like Tamino and Pamino in *The Magic Flute*, she had come through the wall of fire.

In that situation, where they're being critiqued in front of others, some people get angry, while some are terrified and, quite literally, quaking. But here's the thing that's critical to Immersion: you have to show yourself to other people and *ask* to learn about yourself – or at least be willing to listen, as this young woman ultimately was.

We can't judge our own patterns and foibles, because we simply cannot see them. We can't identify all the shields we're holding up, because they are *our* shields and we put them up for a reason. Any one shield might have been a useful protective mechanism when we put it up, but most likely it is now just a bad postural habit – and one that's blocking us, vocally and emotionally. What do shields do? They repel. They push back. They turn people away. But *you* can't see it. And we're terrified of asking anyone. Everyone around us could give us the answers, but it's an 'undiscussable', so we never ask and we never tell. Time to break the mould, I say. You're going to have to ask.

You can do this exercise without me to guide/persuade/ bully you if you ask somebody to help. It should be someone you trust, who knows you well and who will tell you the truth. Ask them to be brutally honest. Anything less and you're both wasting your time. Ideally, you'll do it for each other.

First, do a little show-spiel. Just talk for a minute or two as if you were introducing a presentation. Use something you've had to present in the past, or something you've prepared for a near-future engagement. Now, ask your friend the hard questions about what they heard and saw. Here are a few to consider:

- Did you have to strain to hear me?
- Could you hear my breathing?
- Did my chest lift?
- Is my voice higher or lower than you think it might sit more naturally?

- Did my mouth open?
- Do I have a repetitive gesture?
- If so, is it distracting?
- Did I throw my head forward?
- Was I on one leg?
- Which part of my body moved when I started to make sound?
- Did I make eye contact? If not, where did I look?

Assuming you've picked a trustworthy critic, they'll tell you straight up. They probably know what your distracting bad habit is before you even ask. I should say, this is also the time to recognise what you're doing right. So in your critiquing session, do tell each other what's working.

Another helpful process in this first immersive stage can be to reflect on your life experiences and identify those that might have dampened your ability to enjoy vocal expression. What has influenced your own impression of how you sound? Think about any confidence-crippling incidents you've experienced. For me it was that moment onstage aged five. I couldn't move. Frozen to the spot. I've had that experience many, many times, which might surprise you, but I believe it's rooted in that 'Oh no, they're judging me' moment.

For you, it might be that experience in choir at school. Did someone point you out as the person 'out of tune'? Were you asked to go to the back or mime?

CASE
STUDY

PASCAL'S STORY – FINDING THE TRIGGER FROM THE PAST

'I remember in about Grade 3 not passing the choir selection line-up at primary school. Now that I think about it, what a bizarre process: lining up with all the other kids at the front of the class and singing the national anthem. The fascist teacher (who was probably a nice person, really) marched down the aisle, listening to each of us for a few seconds – and then we were given the nod or the flick! That's my recollection of it, and in writing this I'm thinking about how my inner voice seems sound and strong, but the energy required for me to put my voice into the outer world has always been enormous.'

———

Think about the voices of your parents. I've told you how important the voices of both my parents were to me, in different ways. Even if your parents didn't have especially distinctive voices, their voices and the way they used them are likely to have had a strong influence on you.

Here are some questions to consider quietly. Thinking

about them and answering them in your head as you go will
help you identify some of your blockages and also help you
create your path for change. You don't need to write anything
down – just use these questions as prompts for reflection on particular areas of your life. If nothing comes up for you, move on.

- Can you think of any specific critical incidents in
  your childhood?

- How old were you, where were you, who was there,
  and what happened?

- Did anything change after that event?

- What's driving you to make change now?

- What external feedback have you had to make you
  want to change?

- Do you think you're stuck with the voice you have,
  even if you don't like it?

- Have you had a physical injury?

- Have you had a vocal injury?

- Describe your mother's voice.

- Describe your father's voice.

- Does your family have a vocal style – for example,
  nasal, loud, soft?

- Was there music in your house when you were
  growing up? What sort?

- When did you stop enjoying singing?

- Were you involved in performances?

- Were you in a choir?

- Did you do music lessons?

- As an adult, did you continue with music or performance?

- Why did you stop?

- As an adult, think about your experiences of giving presentations (if you've had them).

- Think about your experiences of participating (or not) in meetings.

In addition to reflecting on the above questions, listen to yourself when you're meeting and greeting people; when you're talking to people in any situation at all – even ordering your regular coffee tomorrow morning. How do you sound? Friendly, open, confident? Defensive? Aggressive? Jocular? Loud? Shy?

The feedback from these three processes will help you establish where you're at now – the base from which your voice will spring.

That, my friends, is immersion. You've discovered what's in your box of tricks. You're aware of what's blocking you, and what you're doing well. And we know you're ready to change because you're here, immersing yourself in study and self-reflection.

You've laid yourself bare and discovered your habitual shields, and you're ready to lay them down.

Incubation

Now let's incubate! Incubation is the part where we learn new skills and develop new patterns.

As we work together to remove those veils and reveal your true vocal power, we're learning about so much more than voice. As you master the practical steps to get your share of voice, other benefits will flow, such as your reactions to tense or stressful situations and how you deal with nerves, and you might even get relief from back and neck pain as we resolve those habitual postural problems. And, of course, you will gain a tremendous amount of self-confidence.

UNLEASHING THE BEAST

Dawn was a human resources manager who came to one of my group workshops, and we all agreed that she had a good sound going. She was intrigued, so she came to me for private coaching to find out some more. We worked together on her breathing and the physical blockages that were limiting her sound. On the very first session, suddenly out came this *enormous* voice. It was a musical theatre voice of giant magnitude. It was incredible. She didn't know she had it!

Sometimes when people first hear themselves like this, they cry. Some people freeze and say, 'What was that?' It's their own voice!

From my perspective, when I've coached them to that point of being able to get their true sound out and when they let it go for the first time (even when it's not the showstopping voice that Dawn had), it makes me shiver.

Dawn had a voice but had never had any singing lessons. So we began to walk – in a vocal sense – step by step. We started with one note, expanded to two, then strung a whole line of notes together. Then we added phrases together with the breath. Then we started to work on correct movement of mouth, and added arm movements, to help guide Dawn's air.

It was exhilarating. Dawn came back to the second session to say she'd had a great experience with her 'new voice'. Oh, what was that, I asked? Well, she had stood outside Flinders Street Station in Melbourne and sung 'The Rose' at the top of her voice. She could, so she did!

We had created a monster – and I couldn't have been more thrilled!

———

Once you've got the incubation phase underway, it's time for illuminaaaaattiion. All right, OK; it's actually illumination. But indulge me: imagine me singing *illllllummminnnnattiiooonnnn* to you, with a happy little trill in my voice.

Illumination is taking all we've learned (and all you're about to learn) and really making it part of yourself. It's time to practise, practise, practise until you get to a point where you're in that elusive 'flow state'. By the time you've reached the top of the staircase, you've rid yourself of those bad old patterns and replaced them with powerful new ones. You've got your vocal flow – musical flow! You are someone with real presence, and you resonate in a way that touches people – and I mean literally. Remember, voice is a physical force, and once we unblock it, we release a whole new you.

The Seven Veils

THE SEVEN VEILS

The biggest mistake you can make when you dream of having greater presence and influence is to think you're stuck with the voice you have.

We are each born with a massive repertoire of sound, and we squash it right down. Some people develop bizarre patterns of body posture and laryngeal posture, which naturally affect the voice, to cover their anxiety about speaking and making themselves understood. Others believe they don't naturally have a powerful voice.

Actually, there's no such thing as a non-powerful voice. It's about how much air comes out of your body, and if you block that air, you don't have any power.

I like to think of Salome's dance of the seven veils as a metaphor for releasing your vocal power. The story of Salome, the daughter of Herod, was set as an opera by Richard Strauss. When I was a professional singer, I was what's known as a Strauss/Mozart singer, so this makes sense to me.

Most people will have one or two main veils to unfasten and cast aside. The first of these, breathing, tends to be a disaster for Australians. We also seal our mouths when we're afraid. And gestures – oh! Most Australians wouldn't dare. But what are arms for?

The Seven Veils metaphor could fit neatly with the Anna Karenina Principle (yes, there is such a thing). Anna Karenina was an all-or-nothing kinda girl: if one thing went wrong, it all went wrong. Theoretically, you have to remove all the veils or nothing will work properly. To this I'd say that, to be released, to have your naked glorious sound out there, resonating – that's the ultimate goal.

I would suggest that you recognise your huge potential reper-toire of sound, and start to take risks and experiment. And here's where thinking about it in terms of veils is better than talking about blockages or listening to the stern Karenina. The veils invite you to enjoy the reveal, to revel in each undoing. So go on, take it one veil at a time.

'I could see voice as an enormous, multi-faceted phenomenon, which encompasses the primary ways we contact and communicate our emotional energy and range as well as our ideas, and one of the major ways our individuality or unique selfhood is expressed by us and recognised by others.'

Getting Business Humming: Personal coherence through vocal intelligence within the organisational context
Dr Louise Mahler, 2005

THE DIAPHRAGM

I'm in a taxi driven by a Fijian, and I ask, 'How do you say hello in Fijian?' And he says, 'Bhula,' and I say, 'Oh, bula.' And he says, 'No, it's not bula. It's bhula. Bhula.' There's a huge blast of air behind each word. And Hawaiians say, 'Alohaaaa.' The Māori greeting, the *hongi*, involves pressing noses and foreheads together and sharing air. And think of *shalom*! There's not an ancient greeting that doesn't recognise this puff of air. And yet many Australians say, 'G'day.' Why doesn't it work?

There's no breath in g'day. It's consonant-plosive. It closes off air flow. A bizarre way to greet people. You can feel the difference when you say hello or hi – these words have an 'h', and a generosity that comes from the sharing of air. We need to recognise that although voice isn't visible, it's a physical force experienced by the listener. It's literally the force of air flow.

The author Paul J Moses (1954) notes that the word 'personality' is believed to have derived from the Latin 'persona', which originally meant the mouthpiece of the mask used by actors (*per sona*: the sound of the voice as it passes through). The ancient Greeks considered the person to be represented by their sound; that sound passed through the hole at the mouth of the mask to reach its audience. Also, the term psyche was derived from an older Greek term, *psychein*, which meant 'to breathe' or 'to blow' (Abram 1996, p. 113), an act inextricably linked with making sound.

So when we're casting off the veils hiding our effective communication, the first one to remove is the veil that stops you giving breath to your speech. Breath really is the element without which nothing else works. Breath is the key, and the key to breathing is to release your diaphragm.

What? What's a diaphragm? Most people have no idea where it is, because we can't see it or feel it. Not only is it there, but it should be springy, elastic and constantly moving.

What is the diaphragm?

The diaphragm is a muscle that fits like an archway beneath your lungs. As it contracts it flattens downward within your torso, creating negative pressure in the lungs, causing air to enter. When it releases, it moves upwards, causing air to be expelled. We can breathe unconsciously or consciously: if you don't think about breathing, your body maintains this life-giving process; if you do think about breathing, you can control the flow of breath, the movement of your diaphragm and the fullness of each breath.

When you combine breathing with speaking, the vocal folds in your larynx are brought close together, and on the outward breath, as the air passes through the vocal folds, they open and close very quickly. The rapid pulse of air as it passes

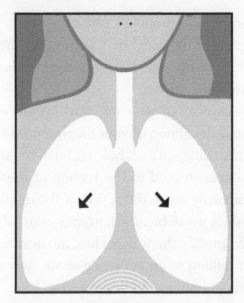

Inhalation – the lungs fill with air as the diaphragm contracts.

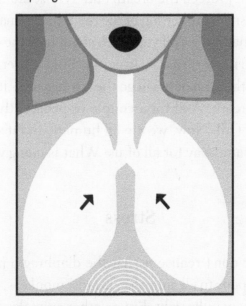

Exhalation – the lungs expel air as the diaphragm releases.

through the vocal folds produces a buzz that is then modified by the other parts of the vocal tract to produce the variations on sound that make up speech. It sounds ridiculous to speak when you're inhaling – try it!

So the availability of your outward breath is essential to speaking, and the action of your diaphragm is essential to maintaining breathing – it's a whole realm of invisible action.

We get so accustomed to the feeling of breathing that we don't consciously sense the action of the diaphragm, and although as babies we all breathe naturally, most of us, usually unconsciously, modify the way we breathe over time.

When I'm talking to an audience about how to improve their use of voice, I always do this exercise. I say, 'Now, everyone, I want you to breathe out.' Then I ask, 'Whose stomach went IN as they forced the breath out? Whose stomach poked OUT?' For a small proportion of the room the stomach goes in, which is the natural way if you think about how the diaphragm is designed to move up as you expel air. But for over two-thirds of the room, the stomach will go the wrong way – it pokes out on the out breath. And for a couple of people, the stomach won't move at all. Now, we are all human, and it's supposed to work the same way for all of us. What is going wrong?

Stress

What people don't realise is that the diaphragm jams under stress. It happens to all animals – lizards, monkeys, everything – the diaphragm pulls tight. But no other animal can maintain shallow breathing the way we can. When humans are born we can't restrict the action of our diaphragms either, and then we develop certain muscles over the course of our younger lives that hold our diaphragms, so that by the time we get to adulthood, during our waking hours many of us are permanently holding them in positions that don't allow us to take, or give, a full breath. The cause of this restriction is usually anxiety. The way we feel about our bodies can also cause us to hold our stomachs in, to present a slimmer profile – but if you hold your stomach in, the diaphragm can't move as it should, you take in less breath, and you give less air out. Your voice will be modified due to reduced flow of air over the vocal folds.

But for the most part, it's repeated or constant stress or anxiety that gradually causes you to permanently restrict your air supply. And for many of us, speaking or presenting in public, whether it's to two or two hundred people, represents an incredible stress.

I've had performance anxiety all my life. If you haven't had it, you don't understand that when your diaphragm jams, it's like being taken captive and tied up. It's not fun.

An inhibited diaphragm makes you look and sound tense

When you jam your diaphragm in an acutely stressful situation, there are two options left to you: breathing high in your chest or rocking backwards and forwards.

Breathing high in your chest is not your best look. The chest is lifted, the shoulders are often raised and you look defensive. Some people rock backwards and forwards when they're making a speech or presentation, which is also what happens when you're in shock. The rocking works as a bellows to move air in and out of your body, almost by force, when your diaphragm is jammed and you can't breathe any other way. As you move your body forward, the air is forced out; as you come back, the air moves in, just enough to keep you alive – but not enough to make any convincing sound.

Both of these options create high muscular tension that is going to squash your neck. You see people's neck muscles standing out to the extreme, with big blue veins that look like a monster from the deep. And as you tense your neck muscles, your throat becomes paralysed, which results in vocal distortion. You sound odd.

Add to this the fact that when you breathe high in your chest, your lungs barely expand, which means you're not getting enough oxygen to fire the major organ of the body, the one that takes the most oxygen – your brain. So when your diaphragm jams with anxiety and you're not getting enough oxygen, it's your brain that suffers the most. Not only do you look bad and sound worse, but your brain doesn't work. You forget what you were going to say. Have you had that experience?

It becomes a negative spiral. I see people all the time who are moving nothing but their eyeballs. They've totally frozen with fear, and they're experiencing the flight response. All they want is to be teleported from the stage or the boardroom or the meeting they're addressing.

People will tell you to relax, but relaxation no longer seems to work for the person in a state of shock. To unlock your diaphragm, you have to do something active.

Unlocking the diaphragm – the first and most vital veil

Stress makes you hold your breath – anything that stresses you will jam your diaphragm. How can you release it?

I have a friend who's a practitioner of Chinese medicine. She said to me, 'You're talking about the same thing we talk about in Chinese medicine. Stress causes a blockage of *qi*. It's a blockage of energy.' *Qi* is the traditional Chinese name for the life force that is essential to your health. How do you get the *qi* to move again? *Qi* energy, breath and voice are all interconnected. Your voice is who you are, and therefore sound is crucial.

Meditation is, of course, one way to help release stress in your everyday life. Find a meditation that works for you. There are plenty of apps. Three months before an engagement, start meditating daily. It only takes a few minutes. I know, I know – if one more person tells you that meditation is what you need, you'll deck them. Say no more.

So there you are in front of me, worried about a performance and experiencing stress, your *qi* all blocked. People have told you to relax. They say, 'You need to take a deep breath in.' The problem here – and it is a serious problem – is that most people have forgotten how to breathe in. You probably haven't done enough meditation to have that control. Instead, the chest lifts, the stomach goes in – it's all back to front. An alternative way I use to unlock your diaphragm and find your voice when you're stressed is to focus on the breath out.

Breathing the *kapalabhati* way

An ancient exercise that's very helpful is *kapalabhati* breathing. You might have heard about it as a yoga practice, and it's a good one to do before you go into a speaking engagement or presentation. It really gets your diaphragm, and therefore your breath, moving.

Stand with your feet shoulder-width apart and your shoulders relaxed, arms out wide, or with one hand resting lightly on your stomach. Now use your stomach muscles to expel your breath through slightly open lips in continuous short, sharp bursts: 'Phe! Phe! Phe! Phe! Phe! Phe! Phe!' Don't even think about your *in* breath. It will take care of itself. Just concentrate on the *out* breath, quickly pulling your belly button in towards your spine to force the air out. As a yoga practice, you would do ten breaths and repeat that cycle three or four times. At an event where you have to speak, three to four blasts of *kapalabhati* practice before you're 'on' will unlock your diaphragm, helping you breathe normally when you speak. It is like pressing the reset button.

The cover cough

When I was backstage at the opera, people would walk around before a performance with their arms out. Picture it: people walking around in ridiculous costumes just going, 'Ah! Ah! Ah!', just initiating sound. They don't do the whole, 'Ah, sweet mystery of life'; they don't do a whole sound or sentence. No. Just 'Ba. Ba. Ba.' Walking in and out of rooms going, 'Hah!

Hah! Hah!', because if you get that sound out you can keep going with whatever comes next. It's just that burst you need to get started.

We did not call it *kapalabhati*. It is just what singers in Vienna did. Of course, you can't do that in a corporate workplace, so, taking a tip from my experience in opera, I started to think about what you *can* do in a work or presentation environment.

Even breathing out sharply can sometimes be awkward at a boardroom table. For these situations, I have devised what I call 'The Cover Cough', because it covers the fact that you're doing an exercise to release the diaphragm, but you look as if you are just clearing your throat. It's socially acceptable.

You have to cough the right way, of course. Some people go, 'Er-her' – well, that won't help. You have to do the right type of cough, a cough where the stomach goes in, kicking the diaphragm into action. There is no need to actually clear your throat, and the chest does not move. The movement actually comes from right down in the lower belly.

The cover cough is your quick fix, your in-emergency-break-glass measure. But you don't want to find yourself in an emergency situation every time you have to talk to a group of people. You can be better prepared and have a more responsive diaphragm by doing a couple of exercises directly before a presentation, and by adopting more regular daily practices in life that will prepare you to easily handle any presentation situation.

Before we go into the serious work, let me tell you how, in the eighteenth century, the castrati were trained to use their diaphragms for maximum effect. Castrati were the little boys who had their balls chopped off so that they would retain their prepubescent vocal range into adulthood. They were forced, as part of their training, to lie on the floor with a pile of books on their stomachs, which they would move up and down with their breath. They'd lie down to get the feeling of the stomach and develop the ability to use their whole lung capacity. It's much easier to do lying down than sitting up. Try it – thankfully you don't have to be a castrato: lift the books for a breath in, drop them for a breath out. No chest movement. I rarely have to get people to do this, because they master it while standing, but sometimes I come across a really hard nut who's got no idea and lying down is the easiest way to show them how breathing from your belly moves your diaphragm and allows you to use your whole breath.

Inspire

During my research I was fascinated to discover that the etymology of certain words hinted back to an ancient understanding of voice. I have already mentioned the words 'personality' and 'psyche'. Another was the word 'inspire'. We use it a lot, but what does it mean?

The word is derived from the Latin verb *spirare*, to breathe. To inspire does not simply mean for you to breathe, but for you to breathe your air into someone else – to inspire them. We have to stop focusing on 'taking' air and, instead, realise that inspiration is the act of 'giving', of giving air that is fully breathed by you and breathed into others to help them breathe.

The message is the medium is the massage

The exchange of breath as we speak is a generous act, and we experience it physically.

The sounds you make as speech are just air coming out of your body and vibrating the vocal folds along the way, which breaks up the air so that it comes out in various frequencies. The faster the vocal folds move, the higher the pitch interpreted by the listening eardrums. Slower vibrations generate lower pitch. If a lot of air hits your eardrum, it hears it as loud sound – that's a greater volume of air coming out at once. Again, it's not rocket science, but it is a revelation to realise that being 'softly spoken' is just about airflow, and has nothing to do with being any less of a person, as we so often assume.

The vibrations you cause when you talk don't just hit a listener's eardrum, they hit everything in the space, or in the room, which is why crystal breaks in response to some sustained notes. I have twice smashed crystal, by accident, just with my voice. The vibrations of someone speaking or singing hit your body physically. Sound massages us.

The flowing voice is the voice of trust

A good masseur doesn't massage in one place, say on your arm, and then abruptly switch to your other arm, because it would break your sense of trust in them. Similarly, speakers who speak fluently and fluidly engender greater trust than those who speak intermittently, with gaps in the delivery of sentences and thoughts.

If I'm talking to you, I need to keep up the flow of air and vibrations – the flow of speech – for you to find what I'm saying trustworthy and believable.

If I constantly break the flow of my voice, stopping and starting again, you don't know . . . when it's . . . coming . . . next. The listener's mind asks, 'Where is this going?' 'What are you doing?' It's discomfiting. We need that constant flow.

After a presentation one day, I was talking to a man who'd been in my audience, and as we spoke, I could tell that he understood what I'd been getting at in relation to the breath. I said, 'You're really good at this, you really get it.' And he replied, 'You know, as a horse trainer . . .' And the penny dropped for me. I ride horses, and they're incredibly sensitive to airflow. When horses greet you, they come up and blow air on you, and they breathe in your air. They can feel it if a fly lands on them. They don't even need to be touched; they feel air moving towards them. I just have to move my hand near my horse's rear end, moving the air towards him, and he'll shift in response. You can move a 750-kilo horse just with this energy.

We too have this capacity. But it is blocked over time. You have to reconnect with the fact that the exchange of air is important. You have to keep breathing while you're speaking. The air has to keep coming out of your body, and the vocal folds have to keep vibrating to hold an audience's attention and to maintain trust. So releasing the breath and unjamming your diaphragm, is the first, most important step in engaging with others.

IN A FEW WORDS

* Your diaphragm is a muscle that fits like an archway beneath your lungs.
* For your voice to have resonance, your breath must flow easily.
* For breath to work fully, the diaphragm must be free.
* Stress and anxiety can cause your diaphragm to jam.
* A jammed diaphragm causes shallow breathing, constricted voice and a lack of oxygen to the brain: you don't look or sound your best, and you cannot think.
* To release your diaphragm before you step into the limelight, use *kapalabhati* breathing (see page 56).
* To release your diaphragm in an emergency when others are around, use the 'Cover Cough' (see page 56).
* To train your diaphragm to function well day-to-day, start meditation practice.
* Flowing breath enables flowing speech, which engenders trust.

Native American greeting

It's been established that when Native Americans greeted someone it was a full physical experience. Their stomachs went in as the air and sound came out – 'Haaoow!' The ancient cultures reflected in Native American traditions suggest that 'inhabiting the full body, the long body, with the voice, may be one of the great soul challenges of adult life.' (Whyte, 1994)

CASE
STUDY

BOB AND THE HABITUALLY SUPPRESSED DIAPHRAGM

Bob was in a senior role in a big firm. Everyone adored him and he was being groomed for the ultimate position. The problem was that Bob had a small voice and no-one could hear him at meetings.

Spot the obvious mistake: There is no such thing as a small voice!

Volume is all about the amount of air that comes out of the body. If you have a habit of withholding air every time you speak, there will only be minimal waves coming out of your body to touch others, to vibrate the ear, to be heard.

It was easy to show Bob how to unjam the diaphragm and make sound. The challenge was that Bob then thought he was yelling.

'Who told you to be quiet and not to yell, Bob?' was the obvious question. So often a parent, a teacher or a peer has done just that.

The way to undo Bob's experience of being told to be quiet was for him to practise, practise, practise making himself heard! I asked him to practise in every possible scenario: in the boardroom, in staff meetings, in corridors, calling out to people in the foyer every day. I gave Bob objective feedback regularly to counter his own gauge of volume.

'What have you done to Bob?' his colleagues smiled. 'He's completely transformed.'

Welcome to the top job, Bob.

———

Can releasing your diaphragm be healing?

Absolutely. I've worked with physically ill people, and some of them would come up to me and say, 'I want to fulfil my dream of singing. You said anyone can sing.' And I'd say, 'Let's do it.' As long as there is no injury, I can get them to sing every time. I just have to manipulate the body. I know everyone can sing; the question is, what are you doing to stop it coming out? So, I do things like this. I say, 'Lean back. I've got your whole body.' Then I get the person to open their arms and make a sound, and I say, 'You listen to that. Hear the difference? It was rounded. It resonates. You feel the walls vibrate.' I'll get them to sing in that position. And if that doesn't work, I'll find another position. And if that doesn't work I'll find another position. It's all about dismantling whatever the blockages are.

The benefits of this exercise are widespread. Studies have shown that breathing high up in the chest can magnify pain, while breathing from the diaphragm can help lessen it. Breathing is an effective source of pain control: breathing high creates unnecessary muscle tension, whereas breathing low actually releases the muscles, relaxes the mind and allows the brain to focus away from pain.

POSTURE

Posture – the way you habitually stand, sit, and hold your body as you move – is instrumental to how you give voice.

Your postural habits might have been formed by fears that are retained as muscle memory – the fear of being taller than your peers when you were a child, for example, can make a grown woman stoop. Some habits might have been formed in response to an injury: if you injure something, the pain will make you avoid using that part of your body, and overuse other parts to compensate. These patterns of fear and compensation easily become habitual, and can result in a tangled bodily creation that is uniquely, sometimes painfully, you.

Ultimately, you need to know only a few things about posture to lift another veil on your ability to speak with presence and influence. Even if you require physiotherapy or other medical interventions to heal various pains, you can still adjust your posture to unveil your true voice.

I call it getting the instrument out of the box. You can't play the violin if it's in its case. You have to get it out of the case. You have to flip the catch, lift the lid and free it.

Stand on your own two feet

Well, who else's feet would you stand on? But there's something in the saying that fits with how much we defer to others and are frequently on the defensive. I find defensiveness often manifests in women as standing with one leg crossed over the other and the hands crossed in front of the body. Think about it. Not only is the body language deferential, diminutive and fearful, but your diaphragm is crushed in, with your elbows across it, your shoulders curled. And without your feet firmly in contact with the ground, you and your voice have no power.

Even more common is that people of both sexes stand with their weight on one foot. It can happen for a number of reasons: they're trying to relax, or mentally taking a step back, backing away from the interaction. It happens all the time in presentations; someone will come on stage to introduce themselves: 'Hi, I'm Joshua,' and the weight shifts back on to one foot, one shoulder drops, the other leg kind of flops out in front – and so does their voice.

You may have noticed that this is an unusual way to approach thinking about the body. Work in this area is normally considered from the non-verbal perspective; that is, the audience/listener will interpret different positions as having certain psychological meanings. Standing on one leg, for instance, says that you do not care. I am interested in this perspective, but more interested in the fact that when you stand on one leg you cannot voice adequately; that is, it is about actually bringing the whole self to the engagement, rather than simply being seen to be doing so.

When you're twisted or lopsided, it's inevitable that your head will come forward to do the 'kemmewnicading'. That's how it sounds: a strangled variation of what your voice could be *communicating*.

Follow this recipe for standing with power and getting your vocal instrument out of its case.

1. Plant your feet, parallel and hip-width apart, and soften your knees.
2. Softening your knees lets your gluteals (those prime-mover butt muscles) engage.
3. This has a ripple effect that gently tilts your pelvis under.
4. This allows your upper back to come into play, moving up and forward so your shoulders can hang loosely from the beautiful framework you've built.
5. The cherry on the cake? Your head, balancing lightly on top of your spine with a long neck at the back.

Yes, there's a bit more to it, so this time, do it with me. Stand up and get yourself into position: Feet parallel, hip-width apart. Feel your weight evenly distributed through your feet. To do this you must soften your knees; feel your weight in your heels, along the outside edge of each foot, in the balls of your feet and lightly in the toes.

Now, engage your butt muscles enough to tilt your pelvis underneath you a little (this isn't a pelvic thrust; we'll talk about that later).

Your genie, your instrument, is emerging from the bottle. Now, everyone can hear that voice in their head that says,

'Put your shoulders back!' Don't. That's so last century. The sensation that will help you stand, walk, talk and look natural and powerful is this: feel the centre of your back, the spine between the shoulderblades, moving firmly through towards your chest. Of course it's not going to get there. But it's the feeling that will help you create a framework from which your shoulders and arms can hang and move freely. In this position, your head can balance, without stressing a single neck muscle, on top of your spine.

Lastly, your hands. What to do with the ruddy hands?! Well, if you can put them by your side, please do, but 98 per cent of people will begin to fiddle under stress. Instead, place one hand on the other wrist (for asymmetry, to draw attention away from the genital area), long and low in front of your body.

It might feel weird at first, your upper back might feel weak because it hasn't done this much work for a while. The fronts of your hips may feel tight because all that sitting we do chronically shortens those muscles – the hip flexors or iliopsoas muscles.

But in this position, your tubes are aligned, your breath can flow, and you're fully powerful.

The test that you're doing it right? I don't want to be able to push you over. I'm not there to give you a shove in passing, but with your weight down in your feet, knees and hips, it should be really hard for me to shift you. It's hugely different to being on one leg or crossed over, where I could knock you over with a feather.

To create this new pattern, you're going to practise every time you're standing in a queue or having a conversation with someone – every time you're standing. And every time you slump your weight on to one leg, the Louise in your head will say, 'No!'

You can cross your hands loosely in front of you, one hand lightly resting on your other wrist. Picture Barack Obama. You often see him standing like this, in rest position. Composed. At ease. Ready to move or initiate sound at any time.

I think of this position as postural 'bar'. Remember playing chasings in the school playground and having 'bar'? A place where no-one could tip you, from which you could catch your breath and consider your next move? Rest position is 'bar', the place from which your voice and your air can flow without restriction. Here you are both open and strong.

So how do you then manage to look professional, rather than stiff? Once you have the right rest position, it's about knowing which bits to move.

A nod to flexibility

When you're speaking, or when you're listening, the head nod is the key to looking open-minded, even when you're standing in a strong rest position.

How do you nod? The hinge is at the top of the neck when you nod forward – you don't lose eye contact with those around you.

Why are we nodding? Nodding the head doesn't actually say I'm agreeing with you. It says I'm flexible of mind, I'm not jammed in my thinking.

When we're defensive, we jam the neck. Police do it chronically and tend to speak in a jammed, tight voice. It's defensive mind, neck jam, strangled vocal outcome. Pauline Hanson does it. So did that annoying person in the neighbourhood of your childhood: 'Oi, what aah yew kidz dewing?'

Nodding unlocks your neck, your fellow feeling and your voice. So when you're listening to someone, you nod with shared humanity, and when you're talking to an audience, you nod to say, 'I hear you,' even if you're going to have to put the opposite case. Even a slight nod helps unjam the neck; it's a movement from which it becomes easier to initiate a response or to keep talking fluidly.

In talking and in listening, remaining immobile is usually a mechanism developed to hide your fear of engagement in a situation: 'Don't see me'; 'Don't pick me'; 'Don't challenge me'; 'Don't ask me a question.'

When I'm presenting, I can quickly tell the responsive people in an audience by their willingness to move a little – by their occasional nodding. It's very different talking to people who sit or stand rigidly. That lack of exchange, of flexibility, can make a roomful of people seem deadly dull.

Ink and Blink chased lions down the stairs!

As in the poem by Ogden Nash, a blink can be powerful. Remembering to blink is a very effective way to maintain movement and the appearance of responsiveness when you're standing still. Of course, blinking too frequently is a sign that you're feeling weak and overwhelmed; but not blinking at all is deer-in-the-headlights stuff – you're frozen with fear. You should blink every four seconds. Counting those seconds can help bring you back into your body when fear has made everything feel surreal. And if you're to one side of the stage or room, waiting for someone to introduce you or to ask you a question, blinking makes you look alert, and just that tiny movement is the start of unlocking your body and your mind, and releasing your voice.

It's a jungle out there and it brings out the gorilla in you

Where women cross their legs and twist their hands in front of their bodies to protect themselves from stressful situations, men frequently respond to stress with primaeval postures.

Men go wide. They spread their legs in a broad stance, maybe put their hands on their hips with their fingers pointing toward their genitals, perhaps scratch their groin . . . Whenever I show an audience my men-go-wide impersonation, I can hear a communal 'Yeeeeesss!' from the women. It's posturing that's memorable for all the wrong reasons.

Now contrast that with someone like Tom Jones, a man with physical presence and vocal power. He shows that 'bar' position – both feet on the ground, butt engaged, back strong – doesn't have to be stiff or immobile. 'Bar' is the perfect position from which to generate movement and a powerful voice: Jones's knees bend, his back moves, his whole body opens up to let his voice – out! There's no questioning his resonance.

It's worth noting the difference between aggression (Jungle Jim) and power (Tom Jones): one is disconcerting behaviour that you want to get away from, the other is anchored, strong and attractive.

Just in case you were wondering: whenever I do my men-go-wide description, someone inevitably asks, 'But what should we do when our boss grapples with himself when he's addressing us?' You don't do anything. What can you do? You might think he's a wanker, but it's not a call to action. You read the move. You say to yourself, 'Oh, that's interesting.' And you make sure you don't do it yourself.

'Naow! That's where yoor WRONG!'

Another aggressive posture is to throw your upper body forward when speaking. If I wanted to say 'No!' with conviction I'd say it from 'bar' position, with an imperceptible pelvic thrust. But people tend to say, 'Naow', and throw the upper body – that's aggression. It's a postural difference, a whole-body attitude. The angle of your neck strangles your vocal folds and it's a one-way street to vocal damage. And not just that: doing so ruins your presence and your ability to influence. Many politicians throw their upper bodies into an argument. They've lost the ability to distinguish between power and aggression, and it does nothing for persuasive argument.

You don't have to be loud to come across as aggressive. Consider the caricature of an accounts clerk. The cartoon accounts clerk has folders under their arm; their body is a little hunched, they take short steps and they say things like, 'Don't get your accounts in by Tuesday, don't expect to be paid.' They're clearly not reaching for the stars of leadership. Compare this to Gough Whitlam, who commanded attention every time he gave a speech.

Remember to stand with feet apart and parallel, knees soft, pelvis under, upper back through, head on but loose, and let your shoulders and arms hang. Where do the hands go? Hands down, asymmetrical, one hand higher, gently holding the other wrist.

And I'll mention this again: people say 'Shoulders back!', but it's not about shoulders back or lifting your chest; you want to bring your upper back through. From this position, not only do you look neutral, but hah! You can speak. You've got the tubes lined up, ready to go.

Remember, if your sound isn't working, it's because your body is crumpled, cramped, crushing your vocal instrument – it's not that anything is inherently wrong with your voice.

Now shake on it

Meeting people can really show your postural poetry in motion.

We all know what a terrible impression the limp handshake makes. The vocal equivalent is to go in with your greeting, bent at the waist and bowing your head, effectively muting your sound: 'Hello.'

A good percentage of people also go in twisted, putting the left leg forward and shaking with the right hand. This just results in a ringing non-endorsement of your presence.

Let your instrument out of its case; maintain your postural alignment. Step in to greet someone with your right foot, reach out your right arm, maintain eye contact, keep your head balanced, and let the air come out with your voice: 'Hello, Bob/Michael/Jean.'

Make sure your head doesn't do the communicating. The comedian Danny Bhoy has a skit describing how Australians tend to go, 'Bob, this is John, John, this is Bob,' with a thrust of the head for every name. The head shouldn't be doing the work; the body should line up and then it's gestures and movement. Keep your body and head aligned so that the air can flow.

I'm always fascinated by the excuses we throw out to justify the blockages we've created. The other day, at a talk I was giving, we were practising shaking hands and a woman put up her hand and said, 'But I am left-handed.' My eyes went skywards. Being left-handed is no excuse for weird twists in hand-shaking. Left-handed people can still shake hands with their right hand. It does not require fine motor skills!

Sitting down

You might have to address people with presence and influence from a seated position – perhaps at a board table, speaking on a panel at a conference, or as a guest on a TV program. Or you might be someone who uses a wheelchair. These skills can be used by everyone.

If you're sitting, the same rules apply as when you're standing, just forget the legs. You're resting on your sit bones, those bones in the middle of each bottom cheek, and your buttocks become your legs. Those butt cheeks are gently engaged, and from there everything's the same. Your middle back is active, your shoulders relaxed. You line yourself up so that the air and voice can flow. It's easier if you're sitting at a table: hands lightly crossed on a table, asymmetrical.

If you're sitting facing an audience from a sofa or a chair, obviously it's important how your body appears. You need to create a visual line. A classic visual line is legs to the side and straight, facing your host or interviewer, ankles crossed, with the back of one knee resting on the other. Body upright, hands asymmetrical, resting on the side of the leg that's on top. It doesn't work to have your legs bent and crossed at the knee, so that one foot is waving at the audience – their view then becomes all about that foot. Your legs have to be to the side.

I feel tremendously uncomfortable in this position, but believe me, if I'm on TV I'm going to do it, because I know it works. Your upper body is straight, because it's still about allowing the body to breathe. Practise. You'll get used to it.

But truthfully, when you sit you lose your power; if you have a choice, stand. Singers don't sit, or if they do, they sit on a stool, because sitting on a chair puts a kink in your vocal power. It's like putting a kink in a vacuum-cleaner hose – nothing gets past that point. So when people tell me, 'We present from a table,' I say, 'Don't. Change it if you can.'

Capture the room

You're not always going on stage; you might just be moving to the front of the room or standing up at a table. If you're getting up from a seated position, be ready; have your vocal instrument lined up, your torso upright. Don't be slumped in your chair – there's nothing worse than handing over to someone who's like a dog on the sofa. Shake yourself long before you're introduced, and have your legs in a position where you can thrust out of your seat – don't bend forward.

When someone introduces you or hands over to you, stand up using your lower body, with your upper body already primed for speech. As you're introduced, immediately do an eye-contact round of the room. Thrust up, out of that chair, with your eyes already engaging the crowd. It sends the message that you're ready, you want to be here and you have something to say. It's powerful, and it's not just power as perceived by the audience, it's power for you.

Compare that to getting up in a bowed position, pushing yourself up with your arms, moving without eye contact to take your place of address. This kind of movement just says, 'Wish you all weren't here. Wish I didn't have to do this.' And it jams your voice down into your tense little rib cage like a canary in a coal mine.

You will notice that we're building up the exercises. It starts with the breath, then goes to posture.

IN A FEW WORDS

···

- Postural habits can be caused by many things; a big one is the stress associated with making sound.
- Such defensive actions can become habits.
- Postural habits can be undone.
- Find postural 'bar' by standing with your feet slightly apart, knees soft, pelvis tipped under, upper back coming through, head resting lightly on top of your spine and your hands gently clasped asymmetrically in front of you.
- Don't 'put your shoulders back'.
- Nod to show that you're flexible of mind.
- Say no, or negate something strongly, from 'bar' position, with your pelvis tilted under slightly.
- Don't throw your head forward – it looks and sounds angry, and takes away your power.
- Keep energy and balance in the lower body to give your voice power; if it's in your upper body it makes you look aggressive and argumentative.
- Shake hands by stepping forward with your right foot, extending your right hand, and maintaining eye contact. Add a smile – why not?
- For great seated posture, rest on your sit bones, engage those butt muscles, bring your upper back through, and let your head rest lightly on top of your spine.
- Don't sit if you can stand – standing gives your vocal system greater power.

CASE
STUDY

POSTURE AND A POLITICAL
STATE OF GRACE

John is a politician. For some reason, John had never learned how to stand and listen. He would wriggle like a man with ants in his pants. He'd put his hands on his hips, then in his pockets, then bend one arm high and hang the other low. The visual impression was a mess; it made audiences feel uncomfortable and influenced the perception of his trustworthiness.

I worked with John to establish his 'rest position', a position that felt safe and looked neutral, from which he would be able to breathe and think. He needed to distribute his weight evenly through both legs – a position of power. He needed to put his head on straight and open his larynx, ready to speak clearly. Once we'd made these small physical adjustments, he was like a new man.

CASE STUDY

POSTURE SENDING ALL THE WRONG MESSAGES

Jackie was the chair of a board. There was nothing about her business she didn't know and she was the perfect person for the job. She told me her problem was that people thought she was intimidating. Jackie was sitting opposite me and, yes, she did look intimidating. Here's what was happening.

Jackie has a 'visual preference' (see the chapter on Eyes, page 113) and over time this had led her to look up, up, up, searching for answers. However, she habitually sat bent forward a little, which brought her head forward, and because she frequently looked upward while thinking, it meant that the whites of her eyes often showed under her iris. Showing the whites of your eyes sends a message of danger.

To appear warmer, Jackie had started leaning even further forward, which made her attitude seem more confrontational – forward body movement can seem aggressive. She thought she'd try smiling more. The problem was that given her forward-leaning posture and the fact she was showing the whites of her eyes, the smile appeared sinister – a spiral to disaster.

The joker in *Batman* comes to mind. Nothing could have been more incongruent. In addition, this head position blocks the throat and Jackie was having to cough constantly to clear her throat (which didn't work because the problem was postural).

This had all become a big problem for her, but it was easy to explain posturally, and once I explained that her visual learning preference had set the whole leaning tower of Pisa in motion, it was easy to adjust her habitual posture to be more comfortable for her and more neutral, even welcoming. Her voice, too, became warmer because she stood and sat straighter, allowing her vocal instrument to work.

THROAT

'Voice is a complex holistic phenomenon, a product which is invisible, made from a place in the body we cannot see or sometimes feel – the larynx – linked to both emotional and physical responses, and with an output we hear differently to those around us.'

This was part of the introduction to my thesis, *Getting Business Humming: Personal coherence through vocal intelligence within the organisational context*. During the course of my research, I discovered many fascinating aspects of voice and the way our understanding of it has influenced us. See whether you agree with this: The act of unrestricted vocalising involves 'opening' the throat.

As part of my studies into voice, in 2000 I attended the Science of Voice and Singing Workshop at the National Voice Centre at the University of Sydney, where Jan Douglas-Morris, a teacher of musculoskeletal anatomy, neuroanatomy and neurophysiology, surprised participants by claiming that 'Not one single muscle holds the throat open. It is as open as it ever will be in its relaxed position.' The point she was making is that the guiding principle is not necessarily to keep the throat open, but to stop it from closing.

Jamming the vocal folds and tension in the throat is a physiological response to a feeling of stress, and sometimes of acute emotional trauma (for instance, see Joan's case study on page 101). This highlights the dual function of the vocal folds: to make sound and to act as a valve to stop the flow of fluid to the lungs – that is, to stop us from drowning.

Larynx: A meeting of the ways

Let's take a look at what happens, physiologically, within your throat.

The larynx, or voice box, is a part of the neck just under your chin. It is supported by rings of cartilage at the front of your neck, where they form the bump of your Adam's apple. The larynx is a crucial juncture: the point at which the aero-digestive tract splits into two separate pathways. Incoming breath travels through the trachea, or windpipe, into the lungs, and incoming food enters the oesophagus and passes into the stomach. An important little flap or valve called the epiglottis covers the trachea whenever we swallow, to prevent food or liquid entering the lungs. Breathing in while you're swallowing can fool the epiglottis into staying open, and you know what happens then – coughing and spluttering at best: fatal obstruction of the airways, or drowning, at worst.

So, there are two choices of pathway into the body. While many people think the vocal folds are somewhere in the throat, they are not. It's important to understand this, to be able to bring the actions of this area under control. Just under the epiglottis, on the way to the lungs, are the vocal folds – two bands of stretchy tissue covered by a thin layer of mucous membrane. These folds form a V, and at the back of each vocal fold is a structure called the arytenoid, which attaches the vocal folds to many small muscles.

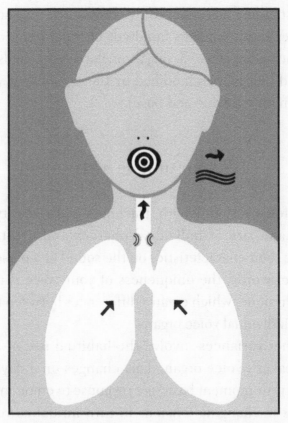

The movement of air from the lungs and past the larynx to create sound.

Like marionette strings, these muscles pull the arytenoids apart from each other during breathing, thereby opening the airway; during speech they bring the arytenoids and the attendant vocal folds together. When you initiate sound, whether it's speech or screaming, singing or a noisy yawn, outward-bound air passes through the vocal folds, which then open and close very quickly. They used to say the folds hit together, but our understanding has changed; we now know they actually roll together and it happens hundreds of times per second. This rapid pulsation of air passing through the vocal folds produces a sound that is then modified by the rest of your vocal tract (your mouth, tongue and nose).

It's your unique instrument

Vocal folds vary in length, thickness and viscosity, and the shape and size of individual pharynx and mouth cavities impose their characteristics on the sound of a person's voice. In other words, the uniqueness of your voice is to do with your physique, which creates differences between the details of the individual voice organs.

Other variances involve the habitual use of a particular speaker's voice organ. This changes on a day-to-day or moment-to-moment basis as a response to emotional stimuli, and these changing tensions in turn influence vocal range and tone.

A lot happens in the throat. It's a bottleneck, if you like, where breath, tension, survival and vocal expression meet.

Looking down the throat of history

In the third century BC, Aristotle proposed that the voice was produced in the trachea and larynx by the impact of air and that this process was carried out by the soul, which Aristotle located in the heart and lungs. In the thirteenth century, there was still a strong belief that the vocal system derived from some emotional origin, this time the heart, even though Claudius Galen, born in 130 AD and considered the founder of laryngology, had already correctly identified the larynx as the instrument of voice production.

As voice became increasingly associated with the throat and specific parts of the larynx, the way voice was depicted in Western medicine moved away from the idea of voice as a magical mirror of the soul, and towards a physiological study of certain anatomical mechanisms. Voice fell from its lofty expressive pedestal to the impoverished position it holds in our culture today.

In fact, voice is inextricable from emotion, and from your soul. It is formed and constantly reformed by habit, experience, new habit and your reactions to life stressors.

Baby, baby, baaaaaby!

In the beginning . . . All of us are born with perfectly functioning vocal processes and, assuming that you have a healthy instrument, in physical terms the permutations and combinations of sound we can produce are limitless.

Some of your speech habits are produced by your geographical and social origin – they can be broadly described as your accent. But also, as we grow, we make alterations that often restrict our vocal tone, range and volume.

Some of those changes occur in the throat. For instance, it is common for many people to retract their tongue backwards down the throat when they feel the fear of singing. Some people do this when they speak as well, but the effect is not as dramatic. The psychological implications are clear – block the passage of air to those around us, block the sharing, block the connection. I knew a woman who had been sexually abused as a girl and who consequently, and understandably, needed to block and defend whenever she communicated as an adult.

We also have false vocal folds: fleshy mounds just above the vocal folds that constrict during swallowing, straining or coughing. They are part of the triple seal (the epiglottis, the vocal folds and the false vocal folds) to the lungs. They pop out, pop back, then pop out again. When they pop out they interfere with the space above the vocal folds, as if they were pressing down on them, stopping them from working properly, and you get varying degrees of repressed tone. At the most severe end of the scale, you can't make any sound at all. On a less severe level, you get a gravelly voice. This can be the voice of depression: monotonal, flat, with words that are hard to distinguish. To achieve full vocal resonance, your false vocal folds need to be retracted back into the lining of the larynx.

Back, false folds, back, back!

What makes the false vocal folds retract? This is a question I often ask, because the answer most people give clearly shows how our lack of understanding leads us down the wrong path. Most people say a cough will do it. A cough can kick your diaphragm along, and yes, it also momentarily makes the vocal folds retreat, but let me tell you that *after* a cough the false vocal folds just spring right on back into their blocking position. The next option is to reach for a glass of water. Go crazy! Drink like there's no tomorrow. Swallowing might help you release, but this isn't a great solution. Turning your attention to drinking might distract you enough for the false vocal folds to retreat from their defensive position. But think about it. The false vocal folds and vocal folds are on the way to the lungs, not the stomach. Any water you drink does not pass by them. This is not to say that water is not critical for the throat. Vocal folds need to be moist, and for that to happen, the body needs to be hydrated. But that means the time to drink water is *before* a performance. Turning to drink when you're supposed to be 'on' is not the answer, and if you need proof of this just look on a professional stage – do actors or opera singers have glasses of water onstage at their disposal?

So what makes the false vocal folds retract? Fascinatingly, it's the muscles under the eyes. When you lift the muscles under the eyes (and the easiest way to do this is to smile), the false vocal folds can't pop out. It's one of those physical-muscular reciprocal deals that also makes complete sense in the emotional-vocal cycle.

Think about how you can hear someone smiling when you're talking to them on the phone. A smile completely changes the tone of a person's voice. Fortunately, this is one case where you can fake it till you make it.

When you're stressed and anxious and your voice fails you, smile! Make your eyes crinkle. Lift those muscles under your lower eyelashes. Your false vocal folds will retract and your voice will be released.

Studies have also shown that smiling, even if it's fake, gives you a little shot of endorphins that can actually improve your mood. Bonus!

Swanning about

You can see why we couldn't go straight for the throat without first considering posture. The way your head and neck are aligned makes all the difference to the shape of your larynx. Everyone thinks the throat is where it all happens, and to some extent that's true, but the throat can't work if it's strangled by a furious neck, or kinked by a curled stance.

There are three main laryngeal postures, as described by New York-based speech pathologist Jo Estill, famous for her work on the conscious control of the musculature of the voice to alter voice quality. In completing the three levels of Estil Voice Training I discovered that:

1. The larynx sits flat, which results in your normal speaking voice.
2. The larynx is tilted upwards at the back for your singing voice.
3. The larynx tilts upwards to the front for belting.

To give your speaking voice the potential for the most volume and power, you want to keep your neck upright – not tense, just naturally upright, which assists a flat larynx.

When you use your singing voice, tilting the larynx up at the back allows the vocal folds to lengthen so that you can hit higher notes. This laryngeal posture allows for volume in high sung notes, but it's less effective when you're speaking in a low range. You've heard people do it: 'Oh hello, deeear.' 'Over hee-ere.' Works well with babies and dogs, but not with people you're trying to influence.

When you're speaking in boardrooms or coaching the kids' soccer, or trying to hold someone's attention, you don't want to be using singing voice. A lot of people do so nonetheless, and it is common for some people who have a Scottish accent or those who are accustomed to using the pitch variations in Asian languages.

And belting? Well, there's no place for belting in the board-room. At one point Spanish flamenco dancers were the only ones known to use it, but belting came into its own with rock 'n' roll in the Fifties: 'You know you make me wanna SHOUT.' It's actually the sound of pain. Belting is screaming. You need to hold the larynx quite high, you tilt the head backwards, and to hold it up, you use your upper body, clamping the upper back to support it. There's a real passion to belting: 'I'm in CHAINS,' 'It's raining men, hallelujah, it's raining men.' (And yet, if you shift your larynx to a singing position, 'It's raining men' can sound like a hymn – not the right mood at all!)

When I went to the Conservatorium we weren't allowed to belt. I'd never belted a note in my life until fifteen years ago, when I did training in Jo Estill's methods. I thought,

'Hell, I looove belting.' But if you don't do belting properly, you can hurt your voice, because at that angle your larynx can get squeezed and be damaged. You've got to get it up above the bend in your neck. One of the best belters ever is John Farnham. 'You're the voice, try and understand it.' Love it!

Why do I know about this stuff? Because it's my problem as much as anyone else's. I've noticed that my voice has changed over the years. I used to be always in my singing voice and I used to speak like that (after all, that's how I'd been trained). But when I started public speaking it was not effective. I've had to train the speaking voice: train myself to use the flat larynx. And my speaking voice has really changed; it's much warmer and more resonant than it used to be. I recently had to take a video of one of my earlier talks off my website, because I listened to it and it was too high-pitched. I don't sound anything like that any more. (Of course, I still play with those sounds, but it's not my usual way of speaking – remember, voice is a choice!)

The voice unplugged – twang!

Voice is just an acoustic phenomenon. Fascinating fact: we all, at the vocal folds, make the same sound when air comes out – 'zzzzzzzzzzzz'. It sounds like buzzing, and we all make it. It's how you shape the section between your larynx and the roof of your mouth – the cavern formed by your mouth, tongue, teeth and lips – that gives you your sound. It starts as a buzz and then we shape it on the way out. That is, it all just comes down to acoustics.

When we make resonant sound the false vocal folds have disappeared, the space above the larynx is open and we have as much space in the cavern as we can get. Opening the back of your mouth wider (like a snake) increases the volume of the space yet again, and that gives your voice the warmest tone.

Or you can move your epiglottis and vocal folds to be as close together as possible, to leave just a tiny gap at the top of the vocal folds, and then open the back of your throat as big and wide as possible. You did this naturally as a baby and toddler, and it gives you what's known as twang. It can be quite acoustically effective because when you have a small hole that then goes into a big hole, it works like a megaphone.

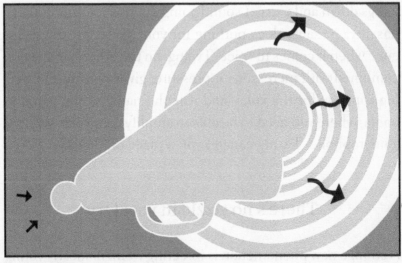

The megaphone effect created by twang.

Of course, it is ridiculous to consider moving your epiglottis and vocal folds in certain ways consciously. However, being able to use twang on demand is important, because it delivers a certain vibration that carries. Fortunately, we can all do it because we were born with this ability to get our mother's attention – 'Maaaum! Maaaum!' It's not just volume, it's an acoustic effect that magnifies the sound in a way that literally carries through various materials. It cuts through walls.

If you're addressing people in a large room or addressing a large roomful of people, twang is a healthy way to get attention.

Australians have a lot of twang in their sound and people call it nasal. It's not nasal. The difference between nasal and twang is worth understanding, because twang carries and nasality does not. When you speak normally, the palate is closed. No sound goes through the nose. But if your uvula hangs down and you get sound going up into your nose, that's nasality. Nasality does nothing for your presence and influence when it comes to voice. Twang, on the other hand, when combined with increased air pressure, gives maximum carrying capacity for the voice and it is the name of the game in opera, where you need to be able to amplify your voice without a microphone. Twang can get you a place on the stage.

There's no sizzle in vocal fry

A strange new phenomenon is infecting women, mostly young women. It's the low-level, gurgling vibrato that says you don't give a damn about anything. 'I don't know why I even go to work,' 'What else can you expect?' and so on. You'll know it when you hear it. It's a modern Hollywood-ingenue kind of thing (and I use the word ingenue loosely). It is the voice used by many of the reality stars, to pop stars like the Kardashians, and I'm noticing it in public life in epidemic proportions. Yes, singers of popular song can learn to use vocal fry to reach low notes, but I don't think they realise that if they use it in speech, they'll never sound anything but bored and boring. It's just a flapping of the vocal folds in the breeze, which is supposed to let you know the speaker is cool. It sends a message that the person doesn't want to engage with you too directly. Some people use vocal fry constantly; others just drop into it to murder the end of any sentence.

Research into vocal fry tells us two things. One is that when you engage in vocal fry, you are using only one-sixth of the air you'd use in normal speech. Now, we know that exchanging air results in 'personal connection'. The amount of air you allow to flow when you speak communicates to your audience how much you are prepared to give and engage. So the obvious implication when you restrict your airflow with vocal fry is that you do not want to connect. Unsurprisingly, research has also shown that women who use vocal fry during job interviews get only 20 per cent of the jobs of those who apply without putting on the fry. Of course, both men and women can do it, but it seems to be women who most frequently disempower themselves with this technique.

Sometimes I go into a suburban shop and a young sales assistant will greet me with a ridiculous, if unconscious, amount of vocal fry. I cannot help looking to the stars and exclaiming, 'Please God, tell me that is not permanent!' If voice is a choice, why on earth would you choose to use something as personally detrimental and destructive as vocal fry?

But let's talk about sex

More fascinating than fry is the voice of sexual attraction. Most people don't realise that the vocal folds also have a sexual function. They respond to many emotions, including sexual excitement, by swelling and lubricating. When both men and women are sexually excited, the parts of the vocal folds that beat together when you're speaking fill with blood, making them shorter and fatter.

This has an effect on pitch. We know that hitting the high notes is achieved by stretching the vocal folds, making them long and thin. Conversely, short, fat vocal folds allow you to generate lower notes.

Also, when they fill with blood, the vocal folds no longer hit cleanly together like scissors in a V; instead their shortened, rounded surfaces only hit at one point, which allows a lot of air to escape between them.

So the voice of sexual excitement has two qualities: it is low and breathy. Think Barry White: 'Where does it hurt, baby?', or Marilyn Monroe: 'Happy Birthday Mr President'.

We've learned how to manipulate our vocal folds to generate these varieties of pitch. But sexual excitement causes involuntary swelling and shortening of the folds.

When you're actually sexually excited, as opposed to putting it on for effect, you can't control the vocal folds; you can't easily make them long and thin again because it takes some time for the blood to disperse. So you lose your ability to generate top notes until the swelling goes down.

Usually, the voice of sexual excitement is associated with caring about and giving to the 'audience', and of course there are degrees of giving and caring. In fact, people invoke a low and breathy sound when they want to show that they care. If you've seen *Kath & Kim*, think of the counsellor's voice. It was hilariously overdone, but this vocal tool is an essential part of the repertoire of the person who cares, in and out of the bedroom.

Increasing your repertoire

My studies of voice science underscored how voice training often includes conscious physical mastery of the shape of the vocal tract for specific ends. Translating that in my work helping would-be influencers in all walks of life has given me a way to reduce restriction and return the voice to its original state – a state of perfect functioning.

In practice, working with my clients in person, I follow a process that begins with helping them free up their breath and straighten their posture, and then incorporating these new more voice-conducive patterns into everyday interactions. It's tricky trying to create or manufacture stressful situations in which people can practise dealing with their stress responses, but here is one way to fast-track stress – try singing. We're all born able to sing and, as I've mentioned earlier, we frequently modify how we use our vocal tract so that singing no longer feels possible, whether it's due to habit, trauma or our reactions to adversity. Recovering your singing voice can have a profound effect on your confidence, your emotions and your resonance. The recovery process is different for everyone, and I won't attempt to go into it in this book.

But just for our purposes here, let's give it a go by singing the simple first line of Olivia Newton-John's song: 'I love you, I honestly love you.'

1. Make sure you are standing up straight.
2. Kick your diaphragm clear with a quick *kapalabhati* exercise.
3. Let the breath into your lower body.
4. Associate that breath, low in your body, with opening your mouth.
5. Sing 'Aaaahh' as you open your arms to guide the sound.
6. Lift the front of your tongue up to the top of your mouth for the 'L' (mouth stays open).
7. Keep singing 'ah'.
8. Bottom lip comes under top teeth for the 'v'.
9. Lips go forward for the 'you'.
10. Keep the air flowing.
11. Use your hands to guide the phrase to a close.

Let me emphasise, though, that the biggest mistake we make about our voices as adults is to think we're stuck with the voice we have now. We are born with a massive repertoire of sound, and we squash it down with our anxious breathing, fearful posture and constricted throats. People are always telling me they don't have a powerful voice. Actually, there's no such thing as a non-powerful voice. It's about how much air comes out of your body, and if you block that air you don't have any power. So I would suggest that you recognise your huuuge repertoire of sound, and start to experiment.

IN A FEW WORDS

- Trauma and stress can cause parts of the larynx to jam, and repeated stress can hold the folds in a jammed and poorly functioning position. This then becomes habitual.

- Your voice is unique, influenced by physiology, geography (accent) and how you use your physiology to produce sound and language.

- You can recognise and undo unwanted blockages.

- Smile to retract your obstructive false vocal folds. Smiling pops them back in and lets your actual vocal folds work more effectively.

- Keep your head on straight to allow the larynx to move as required to alter pitch and tone.

- Want to get attention? Turn your mouth into a megaphone and go for twang!

- The voice of sexual excitement signals the psychology of caring.

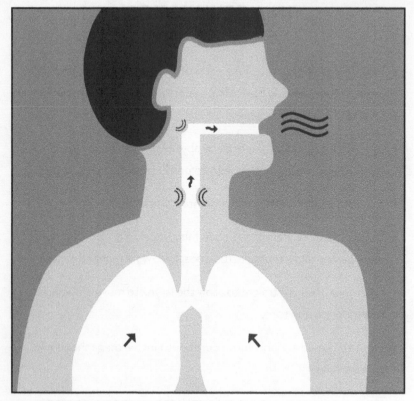

The process of vocal sound: movement of air from the lungs, through the larynx, the nasopharynx and then out of the mouth.

Health and science

Vocal sound, from the perspective of the health professional, is seen as the result of interplay between three parts of the body: the breathing mechanism, which serves as the compression chamber; the larynx, through which tone is created; and the area above the larynx (commonly known as the nasopharynx), pharynx and mouth, where sound is shaped.

In voice science, vocalisation begins when the air is expelled from the lungs along a tube ascending towards the mouth. Passing the vocal folds, which are housed in the larynx, sound waves are created when the vocal folds open and close. This is then amplified by the pharynx and mouth, through which the waves pass.

What's fascinating is that the emotional effect on the larynx can often be ignored.

The common voice

At one interdisciplinary clinic in America, the voice psychologists Deborah Caputo Rosen and Robert Thayer Sataloff work with psychogenic disorders. They took the unprecedented approach of considering not only actors and singers as 'voice professionals', but others, such as 'attorneys, teachers, broadcasters, clergy, salespeople, politicians, physicians, shop foremen, football quarterbacks, secretaries, telephone receptionists and anyone else whose ability to earn a living is impaired by the presence of voice dysfunction' (1998, pp. 19–20). Their approach, unlike that of classical singing, recognises 'every patient with a voice complaint should be treated as Luciano Pavarotti, Tom Jones or Barbra Streisand' (1998, p. 44), accepting the talent of each person as precious.

JOAN'S TRAUMA AND HER FALSE VOCAL FOLDS

I met Jan in a session for executives and she begged me to work with her mother, Joan, who used to sing, but no longer did. I had a session with Joan and she told me it was a waste of time, because she had lost her voice.

So often we have this I-have-been-taken-over-by-aliens approach to voice, as though we have no control or choice, but that isn't true.

I began by asking Joan what her voice used to be like, what it is like now and when she 'lost' her voice. I was listening to her patterns, while also trying to discover if the problem was physical or psychological damage.

She could trace the change in her voice to around four years ago. 'So, what else happened four years ago?' I ask. It turned out that Joan's other daughter had died of cancer, and that Joan had nursed her for two years before she died. This was clearly a nightmare experience.

I explained to Joan that through trauma, we stop breathing and that the throat closes, especially, in her case, the false vocal folds. Over prolonged periods of trauma, this becomes habit.

We did some basic exercises. Voila, the voice started to come back.

The questions arose: Would your daughter want you to be de-voiced now? Does it serve you now to be de-voiced, or will you choose to let the throat be open again? There were tears. More healing. More voice.

I'm not a psychologist, but voice is so entwined with emotion. Sometimes releasing one can help the other, and vice versa.

MOUTH & TONGUE

I had a client called Karen who was a consultant in organisational development – one of the generous people who stepped up as a research subject for my PhD. Here's part of what she wrote about her experience with my methods of releasing the voice.

'I say, "Oh Louise, I'm not loud." Louise says, "Well, let's have a listen. Open your mouth and yell.' I let loose: "Aaaaaahhhhh!!!!" Louise: "Here's a tip – try opening your mouth so the sound can come out!"

'I was so shocked to discover, by looking in the mirror, that what I thought of and experienced as an open mouth was a pretty much closed mouth. But when I opened my mouth – really stretched that baby, well, voila – I was LOUD! Loud enough to give myself a very big fright.

'To demonstrate what's happening with my voice, Louise leaves the room, then tries to come in through the door, which she is holding jammed: she tries desperately to squeeze through the tiny gap left. Every so often she manages to burst through. "That's your voice," she says, "a huge big voice, constantly being held back." She tells me my voice is big enough to bring down the walls of Jericho. I am flabbergasted, thrilled and terrified all at the same time. I have a voice.'

Like the hundreds of executives I have coached since, Karen found the connection between changing her habits and finding her voice. (Read Karen's whole story on page 179 – she expresses the joy of removing all her veils so movingly.)

Everybody *thinks* they're opening their mouth to speak, but the truth is most of us barely open our mouths, and usually, when we do, we shut them again very quickly.

Sometimes I sit in a meeting and look across the table at a row of people. I know one of them is talking, but which one? If there were a university course in ventriloquism, it would be easy credit points for many!

To the observer or listener, a closed mouth is fearful and defensive. So many of us fall right into the trap of saying a few words with barely open mouths, and then shutting them again. Tight. Then letting out the next few utterances. So you get this typical stilted script: 'Hello.' Lips together. 'Nice to meet you.' Lips together.

The complete antithesis to this was Dame Joan Sutherland, who never muted her sound by closing her mouth. Consequently, you could barely understand a word she said, because she never subjugated sound quality to diction.

For people in the habit of breaking the flow of air by frequently zipping their lips, their intended communication is also broken. Frequently closing your mouth sends the wrong message, and it foils the whole physiology for making yourself heard. On the other hand, keeping your mouth constantly open means you make no sense. So if you can't close your mouth too often and you have to make yourself understood, it is the tongue that must get active.

The vibrating buzz produced by air flowing over your vocal folds is shaped into sounds by your pharynx, your cavernous maw, and your tongue and teeth. Like a dancing bear, the tongue is the moving part in all this. It allows the air to keep flowing from between your open lips and massage the audience, hit the walls and reverberate! At the same time, it allows you to make sense.

The simple rule of thumb is to open your mouth to the width of two fingers and exercise the tongue.

Rule of thumb, get it? Hah haaaaah. Laugh! 'Hah, haaaaah' – keep that mouth open and count to four. It feels weird at first, but you'll notice if you do it in front of a mirror, as Karen did, that it doesn't look odd. Think of Elvis Presley. His mouth was always ready for action, open way before he began.

Even if you're just saying 'Hi', your mouth is open, two fingers, before you utter the 'h' and then it's an extended 'Haaeee', with air flowing. Mouth stays open, mouth stays open, mouth stays open.

A great contemporary practitioner of the art of keeping the air flowing is Hillary Clinton, who always walks on stage and goes, 'Thaank yooo, thaank yooo!' She also rarely closes her mouth. You can see the psychology of it: by keeping my mouth open, I'm not blocking my connection to you. Both Clinton and Obama also find ways to keep the air flowing as they walk towards a stage or through a crowd. They're coming through, and they reeeach out to people, saying, 'Oh, Michael, hello, how are you? Andrea, great to see you.' They extend an arm to people as they pass, keeping their mouths open, air flowing.

The psychology of the mouth is all about defence. Close it and the conversation's over – and it's hard to convincingly reopen it.

What are you going to do to keep yourself open? Try talking without closing your mouth. Feel how the further your mouth is open, the more the tongue has to work? You've got it in one.

With your head on straight and your jaw softly open, your tongue can be agile, like a snake.

Snake-charming your vowel sounds

The next key question is: how can we loosen our tongues?

The tongue is responsible for vowel sounds, so a good way to exercise it is by practising your vowels: 'ah, eh, ih, oh, uh'. Singers practise opening their mouths and moving their tongues to the vowel sounds *ad nauseam*.

You can do it a little less often, but do practise daily, saying the vowels of the alphabet, keeping your mouth open to the width of two fingers, and with the sound originating from the back of your tongue (the front of the tongue can stay lightly forward): 'Ah, eh, ih, oh, uh. Ah, eh, ih, oh, uh.' Keep the jaw loose and let the back of the tongue form the vowel sounds: 'Ah, eh, ih, oh, uh. Ah, eh, ih, oh, uh.'

You can also incorporate this exercise into everyday speech.

Consider the word 'hi', which you may be able to say many times a day. 'Hi' consists of three things:

1. An explosion of air in the 'H'.
2. The vowel 'ah'.
3. The vowel 'ee'.

'Hi' is an example of a dipthong, that characteristic of English in which two vowels are frequently written as one. In this case it serves our purpose, because 'ah' and 'ee' are at the opposite ends of the spectrum of movement for the tongue – so every time you say 'Hi', your tongue gets a workout.

A little note about 'e': In Australia, we tend to say 'e' as 'oeee', with the teeth shut and the lip slightly curled, which results in something like 'Hoee, noeeeds moeee' – in case you didn't recognise that it's 'He needs me', only with an acute case of the Jacqui Lambies. There's no air coming out. It's squeezed. And of course it does make the sound 'e', so it's not a capital offence, but what you're doing is blocking the air. Make sure you learn this new way of saying 'e': with your mouth open and the sides of the tongue up on your back teeth.

You want to touch people with your air: 'Good aahfternoon!' And even after you've uttered the 'n', keep your mouth open and count to four.

Think of Robin Williams saying, 'Good morning Vietnaaaaam!' Mouth open, air out.

Raspberry smoothie

Here's another easy exercise you can use before talking. Singers frequently begin warming up for performance by blowing raspberries. Unclamp your jaw, keep it loose, and blow through

your lips like a perplexed pony. That gets the air flowing.
'Prprprprprprprprprprr.' Now keep it flowing and launch into
saying something.

Bite your tongue!

Something I get asked all the time is: 'What do you do when
your mouth is dry before a presentation or a meeting?' Water
seems the obvious answer, but drinking shouldn't be necessary. By the time you walk on stage, you should already be
well hydrated.

Of course, it's natural for the moisture to evaporate from
your mouth when you're stressed, but you don't need to drink.
Instead, try another old opera trick: bite your tongue. Singers
are always walking around on stage biting their tongues. Try it
now. Keep biting your tongue, and the saliva will flow in. You
don't have to go, 'Oh shit, oh no, I'll die if I don't get a glass
of water.' We tend to wallow in self-abuse because we don't
know this strategy, but there it is – bite your tongue.

I like to tell the story of a famous entrepreneur, founder
of a hugely successful business, who was hired to speak at
a conference. Not only did they pay him a huge fee to speak,
but they flew him and his wife to the conference on first-class
tickets and put them up for a week in a very expensive hotel.
I was sitting in the front row, next to his wife. As soon as he
walked on stage, I knew immediately that he had performance
anxiety because his head froze, his eyes started to go awry,
and he breathed high. Just because you've founded a stupen-
dously successful business, it doesn't make you a great public

speaker. He came out on stage and immediately went for the water. Of course it resolved nothing. He was still in the same state. Finished the glass, opened another bottle. It didn't solve anything. He barely said anything coherent.

Later, I was walking out with the conference organiser who had paid him the huge fee, as well as buying him first-class plane tickets and a week in a ritzy resort, and she spat, 'What is he, a camel?'

Lots of people do it. They come on stage looking for the water. Not now! Before the presentation is when you hydrate. Do they have water on the theatre stage? Do they have water in opera? No, no-one has water. It's not the right strategy. Just bite your tongue.

Another barrier to opening your mouth is if you know – because someone's told you or you sense people recoiling in your presence – that you have halitosis (bad breath). This, too, can be fixed. Have yourself checked out by a dentist and/ or a doctor, and keep yourself hydrated. Bad breath is almost always caused by one of three things: gastric reflux, in which the acids of the stomach cause smelly reactions; poor dental hygiene, sometimes resulting in decaying teeth or gums; or dehydration.

And don't forget the other strategy for unlocking the jaw and keeping the mouth open, which I touched on in the previous chapter: smile.

Muscle up on the smiles

A genuine smile is like a one-two punch. Or perhaps that should be a one-two muscle tug. Triggered by a pleasing sensation in the brain, two muscles are roused into action: the zygomatic major, in the cheek, tugs the lips upward, and the orbicularis oculi, which encircles the eye socket, squeezes the outside edges of the eye into the shape of a crow's foot.

The entire event is short. It typically lasts from two-thirds of a second to four seconds. The beauty of a genuine smile? Those who witness it often respond by smiling back.

A genuine smile is called the 'Duchenne smile', in honour of French anatomist Guillaume Duchenne, who first studied the emotional expression of facial muscles. As we have already seen, even with a fake smile, as long as the orbicularis oculi is stimulated, the false vocal folds will back off; they'll shrink back from sitting on the vocal folds. No longer obstructed, your folds can vocalise with more freedom.

But here's the other thing, if you smile in response to stress, your lips part and your mouth opens, and it becomes much easier to speak. In the wake of any muscle contraction comes a release, and smiling works on so many levels: to release speech, to release endorphins and to unleash a positive response from your audience. Smiling makes you more appealing.

Another thing to consider is that a 'Duchenne smile' using the muscles around the eyes is believed by some researchers to work both ways – if you smile like this, it actually makes you feel happier. While this can be seen as controversial research today, when the clown Pagliaccio sings 'Ridi Pagliaccio' ('laugh,

Pagliaccio') at least he knows he will keep his job. Reminds me of the joke:

Question: Do you have to be funny to be a speaker?

Answer: Only if you want to be paid.

While I have read that not all people can smile on demand, you are most likely not one of them. You'll get a far better response and be better prepared to react positively to questions if you say, 'Who would like to ask the first question?', keeping your mouth open and smiling. I tell myself to 'grin like an idiot' because the very idea provokes a smile in me. One way to keep your mouth open is to press the middle of your tongue to the top of your palate, the roof of your mouth. But grinning like an idiot has all those wonderful side effects. You'll be doing the true Duchenne in no time.

IN A FEW WORDS

- Open your mouth to the height of two fingers for better sound and a more communicative air. And keep it open!

- Let your jaw soften from the hinge at the back of your teeth for a more agile response to the world.

- Exercise your tongue by practising vowel sounds that initiate from the back of your tongue: 'ah, eh, ih, oh, uh'.

- Loosen your jaw, keep the air flowing and release the lips by blowing raspberries.

- Hydrate before it's your time to speak. If your mouth is still dry, bite your tongue until the saliva flows.

- Smile to reduce your own stress, to release your throat from the false-vocal-fold stranglehold, and to make yourself more appealing to the audience.

- At the end of your talk, ask people whether they have any questions, assume your 'bar' position and 'grin like an idiot' – proven strategy!

- One way to keep your jaw released is by pressing your tongue to the top of your mouth.

Some people compensate for a clenched and immovable jaw with overactive lip movement. Some people just do the one lip: Bill Shorten moves the top lip. John Howard blows into his cheeks.

Tongue twisters

Work on this on your way to work, or at breakfast with the kids:

> 'What a to-do to die today at a minute or two to two,
> a thing distinctly hard to say but harder still to do.
> For they'll beat a tattoo at a quarter to two:
> a rat-ta tat-tat ta tat-tat ta to-to.
> And the dragon will come when he hears the drum
> at a minute or two to two today, at a minute or two to two.'

EYES

They say to children at school that if they present more, they'll become better presenters. No they won't; not if they practise the wrong things. They'll be worse! It's like muscles; you're either practising using the right one or practising using the wrong one. You don't get better if you don't practise the right things.

Unveiling the eyes takes practice. Now, you might wonder how your voice and your eyes could possibly be connected and what relevance that can have to giving a memorable presentation, or to speaking with influence.

Interestingly, eye movement and vocal pitch are intertwined, as if the neurons of one have been twisted with the neurons of the other, like electrical wires, within your brain.

It's how you're programmed

Here's one way of explaining how voice and gaze are connected. It comes from the study of neuro-linguistic programming, a school of behavioural thought. Neuro-linguistic programming recognises that we all develop patterns of behaviour and can identify what those patterns are and update them.

Now, according to this school of thought, we all think and learn by forming pictures in our minds, and by listening and engaging our feelings. But very early in our lives we tend to develop a preference for one of these ways of filtering information. The basic three are called visual, auditory or kinaesthetic.

While we access information using all three modes, we mostly develop a preference for one of these, and we consistently return to it as our main means of interpreting the world. For each way of perceiving information, you will find you change your way of speaking, your breathing patterns, your gestures, your eye movement and your vocal tone. By understanding this you can bring it under control.

The visual types live and learn in pictures. They'll say, 'I see what you're saying.' If they have to make a presentation, they love PowerPoint. They respond to data displayed as graphs or interactive displays. They gesture high, often playing with their hair. They are more likely to breathe high. Their eyes go high when they think and the voice may well go up in pitch. For many of us, that's the way we live – up high, in pictures.

People with an auditory learning preference are those who say things like, 'Yesterday you said . . .' They can recall the exact words you used. Because I'm a visual, I'll say, 'I don't know what I said yesterday,' but they'll know. They will have recorded it in their brains to the extent that they can repeat your words of yesterday or even last week, maybe verbatim. My first husband could come out of the theatre after we'd been to a musical and say, 'I really liked that second song.'

And he could sing it from start to finish. He was an auditory first preference. People with an auditory learning preference have information that 'rings bells', their eyes go left and right when they think and their voice stays steady under stress.

And then there are kinaesthetic people. They're the ones who'll say, 'Hi Trish, love your hair today,' and 'This is lovely, is it silk?' They're the ones to whom the visuals and the auditories want to say 'Get your hands off me,' because kinaesthetics often go through the world touching everything, and they tend to understand things by doing them. They'll say, 'I don't know what you're saying, I've got to do it.' Do it, do it, do it, or touch or feel – that's kinaesthetic. Their voice goes low under stress, their hands gesture low and their eyes go down and right. Have a look at the diagram over the page for a representation of different styles.

How do you know which one you are? Often you just know. But one telltale sign is where your eyes go when you're thinking, and how your voice simultaneously reacts.

Say you're talking to an audience and you lose your train of thought. Or what if someone asks you a gnarly question? Where do you tend to look when you're casting about for the next sentence, or for the answer?

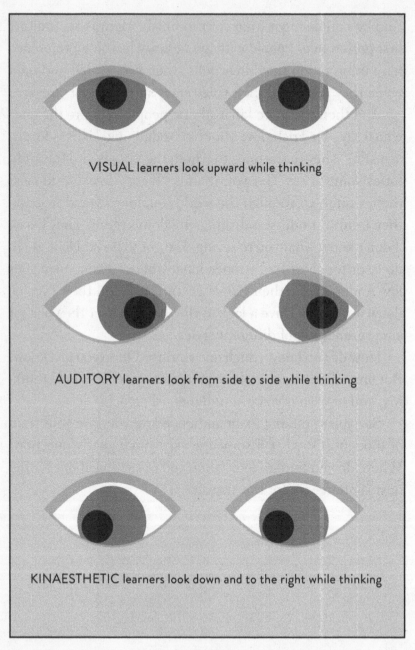

VISUAL learners look upward while thinking

AUDITORY learners look from side to side while thinking

KINAESTHETIC learners look down and to the right while thinking

Direction of eyes during thought based on learning preferences.

Eighty per cent of the time, people with a visual preference will look up, to either side – their eyes will flick up to the left or the right and as they do the pitch of their voices will go up in tandem with their eyes. You can tell that you have a visual preference if under stress your voice tends to rise. Because I'm a visual, if you catch me out with an unexpected question I'll look upwards and say, 'Oh, I don't knowww?' with rising inflection. But if I'm just thinking while speaking, my hands will go to fiddle with the hair on the top of my head, my eyes will look up at an invisible cloud. Eyes go up, voice goes up, hands go up.

Another problem for those with a visual preference is that the voice of leadership is perceived to be deep and low, and the voice of a stressed visual person goes high. Although I'm not going to lower my voice to be seen as a leader, I don't want to send it up higher than it is, either – particularly as a woman, because women's voices are already an octave higher than those of men. If the voice of leadership is perceived as low, giving in to my preference is not going to get me anywhere.

Joe Hockey is a visual, and he gets away with talking in a higher pitch when he's stressed because he's a man. But a woman? The minute we go higher, we go into child's range, and that's when someone's going to say, 'Can I speak to the manager, please?' So you have to be aware of this and avoid doing it.

A variation you'll see quite frequently in those with a visual preference is that some close their eyes to think. Others go out of focus, so they look as if they're looking, but they're actually off in their home zone, ransacking the cupboards for the next thing to say.

Auditories look to either side, at the same level as their ears, and their voices, even under stress, stay in the mid-register. John Howard has an auditory preference, and you'll remember that whenever he was being grilled by the press, his eyes flicked left and right.

People with a kinaesthetic preference look down, they gesture downward with their hands, and their voice also goes down when they're thinking or anxious while speaking.

When you're presenting or trying to engage an audience and you look away from them and your eyes go into your preferential zone, suddenly you're going into your own world. The audience floats off like a piece of driftwood on the tide of their own daily pressures and starts looking at their phones. And it is very difficult to hold your voice steady if you can't steady your eyes. The two go together.

In the realms where you want to have presence and influence, you need to know what your preference is, and then manage it.

Leaving voice and presence aside for a moment, you should know that recognising what preferences other people have can also be extremely helpful. For example, consider that universities are full of visuals, MBA programs are full of visuals, executive teams are full of visuals. Why? Because visual thinking is fast. These people tend to play to each other's preference by doing a whole lot of PowerPoints and saying, well, this is our world. They send their sales forces out into the more diverse population with all that visual material, and a lot of people will switch off. In so many situations, we end up wasting our efforts because of our own preference and our inability to understand that not everyone experiences the world with the emphasis that we do. If you can tailor your message, present it in a way – aurally, with attention to actions, or visually – that suits the people you're presenting to, you'll be way ahead of the crowd.

So how does this tie in with vocal skills? People will notice it if your eye movements seem inconsistent with what you're saying, and they'll interpret this as shiftiness. Even if they don't exactly think you're a liar, they'll doubt the veracity of what you have to say. In Western culture the rule is to engage people with your eyes whenever you're talking. I am told that in many Australian Aboriginal cultures, in complete contrast, you look away for respect. The key is control.

Eye-eye contact for captains going up in the ranks

In Western culture, the most important use of your eyes during any conversation where you want to effect an outcome, or in any presentation during which you want to hold people's attention (is there any other kind?), is to engage with the eyes of your audience.

This can be hard if speaking makes you nervous or you're trying to find your voice. The instinct is to look away, to gather your thoughts, to retreat into yourself, even if only for a moment.

Each of us knows that's the instinct, yet when we're watching and listening to someone speak, as listeners, we read wandering eyes, eyes that flit here and there, eyes that look down, or close in thought, as signs that the speaker is shifty, untrustworthy, obfuscating, unreliable; that they're somehow not speaking the truth. And if you break eye contact frequently, we'll lose interest entirely. Tough, but there it is.

And it's the same theory as with air: break the flow of air, break the trust; break eye contact and the same thing happens. People go to shake hands and look down, look away. It ruins the opportunity to convey your trustworthiness.

There is nothing natural about holding eye contact. Nothing. However, people perceive it as broken trust when you look away, so you have to hold.

And you can't just hold contact Julie Bishop-style, which was fixed and staring in her first several months of office – she was famous for it. (In men, such fixed staring is said to be characteristic of psychopaths, and we definitely notice there's something wrong, whether it's men or women doing it.) Instead, you've got to hold and blink, which gives movement so that people don't know you're holding your eyes. And yes, it hurts, so you've got to practise it until it doesn't hurt.

Julie Bishop has stopped staring fixedly at the camera or interviewer. She's been practising, working on engendering trust. Remember, the amateur practises until they get it right; the professional practises until they can't get it wrong.

And the muscle to exercise in this instance is the one that keeps your eyes engaged, even while your brain is screaming: 'Don't you know I can't think when you keep looking at people! You can't look someone in the eye and expect me to think at the same time, you idiot!' It doesn't take long to get that inner voice to shut up; research says it takes around two minutes of practice at first, and then a little less every other time you practise until it's no big deal at all.

You'll hear all kinds of weird strategies for looking at your audience. Some people will say, 'Focus on people's noses,' or 'Imagine them in the nude.' If this works for you, good luck. There is, however, something sinister about doing this; it undermines your co-communicator. Instead, just look in their eyes ('not around the eyes, but in the eyes', as the hypnotist says in *Little Britain*).

Another strategy I've heard came from a woman who was speaking at a Women In Leadership program. She said, 'Right ladies, let me tell you the trick that I find very successful. When someone is a problem in a meeting, I don't look at them. I look just past them. And I look just past them until they shut up. And then I talk very softly to bring the power back to myself.'

I was sitting there, twitching. What she's describing is an extremely aggressive strategy. It is a strategy we use in desperation for power. Put it in the basket of tricks, but do not bring it out regularly. It is dangerous. Women have enough trouble being heard without speaking softly for effect. Instead, share the breath, speak with power and control the eyes (thus helping the voice).

Perspective works in your favour

When you're facing a whole lot of people, perspective comes into play – and that's very helpful. Down the back of the auditorium or assembly someone might say, 'Oh, she was looking at me the whole time!' Actually, you were looking at 200 people the whole time. Perspective melds the people further away into large groups of one. That is, they say every person in the front row is one person. Every two people in the second row is one person. Every group in subsequent rows becomes one person, until you get to the back few rows where 200 people become one person. With an audience of 1500, you still have to spread the love. Down the front, everyone gets a look, in middle distance even if you're looking at one person, twenty people will think it's them you're talking to, and your eyes must seek to engage, section by section, with the whole crowd. Everybody gets a look.

And it's not just a sweeping glance. You should hold eye contact with one person or group for the duration of each thought. Some people say it's for three seconds and it can work out to be about that time, but, essentially, aim for one look, one thought.

It's the same whether you're in a staff meeting, or making a toast among family and friends at Christmas time. Unless it's a crowd, everyone really does get a look. If the meeting is long, or you're giving a eulogy, you do the zig-zagging rounds. Everyone gets a look.

That's really hard, because we naturally want to look at the person who's smiling at us.

You want to get everyone smiling

You know how most of the barriers to being an influential speaker are just habits that you have to break? Looking at the people who are responsive and smiling at you is a natural reaction. You still have to overcome it and cast your net wide.

In fact, the trick is to look a little more frequently at the person or people who are not smiling at you – to draw them into your magnetic circle. They're the ones you give the extra eye contact to. Recently I was addressing a huge group of people, and there was one lady who was sitting with her arms crossed and scowling, literally scowling. And I thought, 'I'm going to get you.' I constantly returned to her and the next thing you know, she was laughing, and I thought, 'OK, we're off!' If you can crack that nut, then you know you've got the bunch.

I can tell pretty quickly who to focus on when I scope the room from the stage (or from backstage if I can). I look at everyone's faces and I think 'Right! That's the one I have to get,' and when I get him or her I feel good. It encourages me to keep going, so it's worth putting in that effort. It's such a buzz, it'll be worth it to you, too. You've got to get everyone's eyes, draw everyone in. It'll be a challenge, because it's harder to look at the angry, grizzly ones.

Beauty is easy to behold

That's right. Terrible as it sounds, our eyes seek out symmetry and attractiveness in others. There was a stunningly handsome man in the audience the other day and I found myself constantly coming back to him. There was also a very unattractive guy and I made myself gather him in, directing comments to him, such as, 'You'd know about that, Michael.'

You want to look at beautiful people, you want to look at people who smile at you, and you have to overcome that. It's a discipline.

Rank and file before rank

The other classic reflex is to address all your comments to the boss. You're doing the quarterly results presentation to the management team. You say, 'I'd like to show you what the mergers and acquisitions department has achieved since July 1,' and your eyes go straight to the CEO. Don't belittle yourself by looking at the boss! You probably know you're doing it, and it's such a giveaway that you're trying to impress her or him. It's just lack of discipline. Tragic. Get off! Off! I'm pushing you off the stage.

Of course there will be times when the power broker in the room will need added attention. However, mostly you'll gain respect if you treat everyone in your space with the same level of attention; embrace them with your eyes – you'll be everybody's hero, and your department, the management team, your classroom, your personal training group, everyone who comes within your aura will be on board.

Practise, practise, practise until you can't get it wrong. You can't do it in a mirror. You have to practise with living things. We can all sing in the shower, we can all speak in front of the mirror. We've got to do it with the cat, with babies, with people in the post office queue, with staff in a clothing store, with people on the art committee. There's something in the subconscious that needs the living context. There's no challenge in the mirror. Kids are good – try engaging three or more children, getting them to do what you'd like them to do, using words and eyes.

Blinking is your soft, safe haven

Remember we talked briefly about blinking in Posture on page 70? It's that tiniest of movements that, like nodding, makes you look animated even when you're standing still in rest position.

Of course, it also softens your gaze, so that eye contact doesn't become staring – especially when your audience is made up of one or just a few people. It stops your gaze from seeming psychopathic. Psychopaths don't blink.

Blinking makes constant eye contact sustainable: maintaining it isn't natural, but blinking can give you some relief until eye contact becomes habitual for you.

Blink. Some say every three to ten seconds. I learnt fifteen blinks a minute (about every four seconds). Blink and the world blinks with you.

Get out of jail free!

Of course, you can't look straight at other people 100 per cent of the time, and there are two of what I call 'eye escapes' that will be useful to you.

Firstly, you can ask permission to look away. For example, you can respond to a question with, 'I'd have to think about that,' and look away. That's asking permission, and the audience then knows you're taking a moment to consider. This does not break trust.

Or you can look at an object, such as a pen, and say something like 'I've also been considering . . .' You don't break trust when you're clearly looking at something that the audience can also see, because the audience knows what you're looking at. This tactic can easily buy you a little time to find your next thought without scuttling the rapport you've built. But when you look up and to the left and go 'Uuuummmm', the audience doesn't know what you're looking at; they don't know where you've gone.

As someone with a visual preference, I practise holding my gaze level even when I'm on radio, because it controls my voice. If I go off with my eyes, following my thoughts, my voice follows my eyes. It goes high and I sound less credible and authoritative.

In theory, when you're at home with family, or at dinner with friends, you can let your eyes and voice do whatever they will. In practice, practising on everyone will bring you results in every situation – you and the things you have to say will be more memorable. And you will have formed a new and useful pattern. So when it comes to that TV interview, when the cameras are on and someone asks you a tricky question, you can look right at the interviewer or television host and your brain will function, your voice will hold and your answers will ring true. The daily practice required to achieve that kind of discipline is worth it.

Remember, when you feel you want to look away, you blink. The eyes stay still, but blinking is the answer. It makes maintaining eye contact bearable. The other thing you do is you nod. And the third source of relief is smiling. Notice that bringing some kind of movement to every situation where you need to hold still makes it easier, more fluid, keeps you breathing. When we're talking eyes, there can be a lot of movement, but no breaking of contact. Eyes on your audience: that's the game.

IN A FEW WORDS
·····································

- It is natural for the eyes to move.

- Knowing your learning preference can suggest where you will look when you're searching for the words or thought you want to deliver. Most commonly:

  - Someone with a visual learning preference will look up under pressure, and their voice will also rise.
  - Someone with an auditory preference will look left or right when stressed, but their voice will tend to remain unchanged.
  - Someone with a kinaesthetic preference will look down, and their voice will also go lower under stress.

- To engender trust, look directly at the person or people to whom you are speaking.

- Hold your gaze, maintain eye contact with the audience and your voice will remain steady, too, at least in pitch.

- Maintain softness in your appearance by moving your face – nodding, blinking or smiling.

- The most effective softening technique is blinking, because it makes eye contact bearable, and prevents you from looking like a psychopath.

- Blink fifteen times per minute to look attentive.

- Remember the two eye escapes. Ask permission to look away: 'Let me think for a moment how to express this.' Or, if you must look away, look at an object, such as a pen – the audience knows what you're looking at and trust isn't broken.

Interesting fact enters stage left, riding on a pony

If you communicate to a horse that you want them to go in a certain direction, you point and send your eyes in the same direction as you are pointing. If you let your eyes come back to the horse, the creature interprets that as a sign of weakness; you have to hold your gaze in the direction you want them to go. If you let your eyes drift back, they go, 'Oh well, you're not the leader.' Crushing! You have to say, let's go there, and send your gaze in the direction you want your horse to follow.

MOVEMENT

Walking on stage is an opportunity to release yourself – your diaphragm, breath, tension. Think of Barack Obama. He walks on stage with one arm raised. If it's a long walk, he might change arms. It's not just to draw the audience's attention, although it does do that. It's not just to embrace the audience with a wave and draw them to him, although it has that effect too. It releases his body, gets his arms away from his sides and allows the diaphragm to move; it prepares him for the breath that makes speech flow.

If feeling tense causes you to unconsciously move energy to your upper body, it's not a matter of getting rid of that, it's a matter of redirecting the energy back down into your lower body. You do want to be powered up, you do want to be pumped, but be sure to put it into the muscles of the body that can take it. The muscles up around your chest, shoulders and neck can't, and they'll block your voice with their tension. People say, 'You want to relax.' No you don't! 'You want to get rid of the nerves.' No you don't! You want to embrace the energy and redirect it into the bits of the body that can handle it.

My teacher in Austria, Professor Müller-Preis, used to say, 'If you've got a performance, the best thing you can do just beforehand is to run round the block and come back. Move your legs, move your legs, move your legs.' So if I'm really stressed before a performance, I'm not sitting around! I'm moving downstairs, upstairs, walking up and down a corridor at the venue, outside the conference room. If I have to be sitting, waiting to get up to speak, I'll be moving my legs surreptitiously. By moving, you're telling your legs that they're a part of this. Movement is your friend.

As we said in Posture on page 66, the power is in your lower body. Engage your lower body – the best way to do that is with movement – and your upper body is freed. Move your arms away from your torso, and your breath can flow from your belly, over your vocal folds and into the room.

Take the stage with energy, move your legs, raise your arms, let the breath flow.

Arrive at the power position and stop. 'Hello Brisbane!' You can still hear Obama's voice res-o-na-ting!

Architectural design

It's important to plan how movement will continue to drive your voice, your message and your influence. Moving at strategic times will facilitate the voice of trust.

'What next?' I hear you say. 'I can't just walk up and down! That would be annoying.' And yes, it would be, but that is not what we're doing.

Call it choreography, call it blocking out squares, it's a plan to anchor each part of your talk to a part of the space you're working in. I call this architectural design of your space. Importantly, this movement plan also allows you to jog your memory the smart way.

We can assume that you're familiar with your topic, you know the message you want to get across and what you want the audience to do with that information. Now it's time to think about what the accompanying movement-to-speaking connection looks like. It shows you where you'll anchor each element of your presentation, speech or talk.

Here I'm going to use an example we worked through in a recent weekend retreat I did for executives who wanted to improve their presence and influence.

Claire came up to centre stage and gave her introduction: 'Hello everybody! I'm Claire from Wallara Shire Council, and today we're going to spend fifteen minutes together exploring public art.'

Note that Claire did not say any more than she needed to. An introduction needs to be clear, precise and snappy. Everyone wants to waffle and explain more at this point, but it detracts from your ability to influence.

From centre stage, Claire then walked to her right, never losing eye contact with the audience, as she began her story, which concerned a topic close to the heart of the audience. It was about an AFL club which was in the news that day for acquiring a new player, who was going to revitalise the club, attract new fans and help the club start winning games. She told the bulk of the story, which was short – it took no more than a minute – on the right side of the stage, and then began moving back to centre as she made the connection to her message: 'And just as the player is going to revitalise Fitzroy in the league table . . .' now she was back at centre stage, '. . . public art is going to lift our profile as a shire people want to live in.'

You can see from the diagram that the key message always comes back to centre stage.

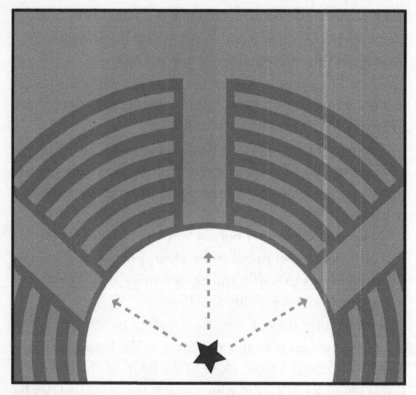

Movement from centre stage (key message delivery) to outer stage (stories) and back to centre stage (reinstating key message).

Note that she did not say 'I'm here to talk to you about the importance of public art.' That's an attention negator. You want to address what the audience is going to do, think or buy, not what you are going to do. Can you hear the difference? One approach is engaging, and already has the audience participating. The other has them wondering whether they've missed the stir-fry at the canteen.

There are a few pre-anchored spaces in every room. One is the power or teacher position in the centre of any given performance space; another is the facilitator position at the side. Claire used these effectively. You can then use other parts of the room to anchor the points you want to make.

From centre stage, Claire moved forward to front-left of stage and began her first argument for public art. She then moved to the other side of the room to explain her second powerful reason for funding a public art program. And for her third compelling argument, she moved into the audience.

She then moved back to centre stage and concluded with something like: 'You can see why public art can become such an attractive addition to our public and inner lives.' She summarised, gesturing to the three places where she'd given her arguments: 'It showcases the talents of people within the community, it engages community opinion, and it adds visual stimulation to our public parks and squares.'

To close, she circled back to the beginning and cleanly finished her engagement by moving to the right again and recapitulating her story about the AFL, saying 'Player X is no guarantee of revitalising your club.' She then moved back to the centre to slam home the fact that public art, on the other hand, is a certain winner.

Then she moved left of centre and said, 'Does anyone have any questions?' She adopted 'bar' position, smiled and kept looking at faces in the audience, she kept her lips parted, not closed off to communication, but keeping the air flowing. Once she'd dealt with questions, she moved back to centre stage and recapped the importance of public art, said the move to start a public art program would be tabled at the next council meeting, and that she would like to see the audience there in support. 'Thank you for your interest in public art, and for your time tonight.'

Can you see how this mapping of the space serves both to remind you of the flow of your talk and to reinforce it for the audience? The message, the story and each vital point have their place. Questions have their place. Anchoring your thoughts is an incredibly useful tool and it frees your voice in two ways. First, it keeps the air and voice flowing because you're moving, using your legs, your large muscle groups, and releasing your body as you go; and even though you might stay in one area to deliver each message, point and story, you can and will move within those anchored spaces too. Second, it frees you from those terrifying moments when you freeze, thinking, 'Where am I up to?', because you're following the map, constantly prompted by the choreography.

When you assign each component of your talk to different areas of the stage, you have an instant and easy-to-follow plan for delivering what you want to say.

I never use notes, because my stage plan cues me to talk about different points of my topic.

It's not a new trick; they did it in Ancient Rome. The Ancient Romans presented in forums with columns.

The columns represented different gods: the goddess of love, the god of war and so on. And speakers would structure their talks, their arguments, their exhortations to fight or till the fields, or whatever message they wanted to propagate, by referencing the relevant columns. They spoke for hours, and they never had notes, because the structure of their talk was already written in the space on the stage.

Anchoring spaces with ideas, or the component parts of your talk, works for people who are listening to you, and it works for you because it's a technique for remembering and for keeping your air flow moving.

At a table you can do the same thing. You set your body up in rest position on your seat but slightly back from the table. When it's your time to talk, you move your seat in, not leaning over the table, but moving forward to take the space: 'Hi, I'm Robert, and we're going to take ten minutes today to go through the quarterly financial results. This quarter, the financials are down on the previous three months; they've been influenced by three factors . . .' and you map out the three factors, with your hands in three sections of the table. You might sit slightly back to take questions, and come forward to the message position (centre stage) to summarise: 'So we understand why this quarter is looking a little soft. The three things to keep in mind will be x, y and z,' as you gesture to those places on the table where those points 'live'. 'Thanks, and let's try to move those numbers north for next quarter.'

You can apply this choreography, this 'move, breathe, talk' strategy to any kind of presentation, talk, address, tribute, speech, eulogy . . . And you can adapt or alter it, once you know what you're doing.

A funny thing happened . . .

I went to see Billy Connolly the other day; I was very keen, because he has always anchored jokes in different parts of the stage. He would say, 'Have you heard the couch joke? Let me tell you the couch joke,' and he would literally walk over to the imaginary couch. He used to mentally map his whole stage; he could see different jokes in their places and he would move to them.

Now Billy Connolly has cancer and Parkinson's Disease, and on this occasion he stood still for two hours. Amazing. Entertaining? Hilarious! Razor-sharp.

When I was working in quality control at BHP, I often heard the expression, 'In God we trust. All others use data.' In this area, it's, 'God (and Billy Connolly) can stand still. The rest of us have to move.'

IN A FEW WORDS

- Prepare for any talk by moving if you can: walking fast around the block or up and down stairs.

- Step up to the stage with energy.

- Architecturally design your engagements.

- Anchor each part of your talk in its own space, whether you're at a lectern, at the front of a room, on a stage or at a desk. And move between spaces.

CASE
STUDY

THE LIVING, BREATHING, MOVING SPEECH

Chris was a CEO, frequently tasked with facing investors and a media scrum. When he had to present to the company's global AGM he said he felt tight. Who wouldn't!

We worked on using small moves to the left and right to signify different aspects of his presentation. We anchored his speech in an easy architecture of spaces. He moved slightly to the side to ask for questions. He turned towards the person when a question was asked. He moved slightly to the other side to describe a metaphor to shape his answer. He returned to the power position, front and centre, to drive his answer home.

Chris found he was able to use these meaningful changes of position to move his body, to feel free to speak, to stop feeling constrained. And he told me, 'It felt fabulous' after putting this strategy into practice just once. Even small changes can make a huge difference.

GESTURES

Many people tell me they've been criticised for gesturing too much. Now, let me explain why this can be helpful, in a roundabout way, with reference to some of the things we've learned so far.

You might have been told that you speak too fast when you're addressing an audience. Actually, there is no such thing as speaking too fast. Research suggests that the faster you speak, the greater your credibility (obviously there are limits, but only when it's extreme). So when someone says you speak too fast, that's their perception, but actually it's more likely that you're not breathing when you speak.

We are influenced by the actions of people around us. You know – when you're looking at someone yawning, you yawn too. Apparently it's an ancient act of empathy. Similarly, everyone needs to pause for breath while they're speaking, and when you're speaking and nervous, it's likely that you're not doing so. Because your audience is unconsciously imitating your bodily actions, they will feel that sense of breathlessness too. Because it's unconscious, they'll grasp at the more obvious manifestation of what's happening with you and interpret it to mean that you're speaking too quickly. So if someone says you talk too fast when presenting, take it kindly, as a hint that you need to breathe. Don't slow down your speech; your speech rate is part of who you are.

Another criticism people make of presenters is that they move around too much. Again, you can move around as much as you like, but your movements have to make sense to the audience. The choreographed, or architecturally designed, mapping of space and moving between areas anchored for different points we want to make – as we discussed in the previous chapter – is exactly what you should be doing. So when people say you move around too much in front of an audience, what they perceive is that your movements are disorganised. They don't make sense with your narrative. Again, it's a criticism you can use constructively. Don't, for goodness sake, stop moving, but do practise the mapping of the stage we outlined in Movement (see page 133).

Now, when people say you gesture 'too much', or 'too wildly', it's unlikely to be the case; it's probably that your gestures don't match what you're saying. They might be incongruent, or you might be using the same gestures too often – they're repetitive. Of course, you don't glue your hands to your sides and never gesture again. You say, 'Thank you! That means I have to think more about the congruence of my gestures.'

Gestures are so, so useful. One of the most important tools in the box. Hands not only help you express yourself and reinforce your message, but they are a wonderful, relevant way to keep your body moving and to guide your air flow.

Beware, though. Once you read the next section, it will

drive you NUTS when you're watching people who aren't aware of all the amusing patterns of gesture we use when we're speaking. In this case, knowledge is . . . humour. If you decide to change your gestures from meaningless repetition to congruence, knowledge will become power.

Knowledge is humour

Each of us has a repetitive gesture with which we are most comfortable. Here are a few of the funny gestures I've observed – and may even have used myself over time.

The flashing fig leaf
The flashing fig leaf has your hands crossed in front of your genitals and one of them opening and closing to flash your crotch in time with your speaking, or for emphasis.

Tyrannosaurus Rex
So many of us do it: we jam our elbows into our ribs, lift our hands high in the middle of our chests and gesture ineffectually with our hands around the level of our sternums – see the dinosaur's little front legs? Incongruent.

The penguin
A classic trap for people who've been told they gesture too much, but some of us do this for no such good reason. Your arms are hanging by your sides, and you just flap your hands to gesture, down there, around your upper thighs.

Windshield wipers

This can destroy the attention of your audience in a few fell swoops: the elbow of one arm rests in the hand of the other; now the loose forearm waves from left to right. Elbows are generally held close to the ribs.

Juggernauts

Perhaps one of the most common gestures used by men and women alike, 'juggernauts' has you holding two large imaginary melons in front of you close to the body, and jiggling them left, right, and sometimes together, to explain concepts.

John Wayne

A true crowd pleaser, this involves thumbs hooked into a belt (although some people don't bother), and fingers clearly pointing to the genitals. Can be one- or two-handed. May involve a hip thrust. A virtually essential ingredient of jungle behaviour (see Posture, page 71), it really is pointing out the obvious.

Such gestures can be hilarious. Sadly, they also make attention levels take a dive. When you get up in front of an audience, everyone wants to hear you. When you take the floor, everyone says, 'Good morning.' 'Good morning.' 'Good morning.' And then you do something weird like Tyrannosaurus Rex or John Wayne, and people disengage. They're still sitting there pretending they're looking at you, but they're actually not. They've mentally left the building.

At best, repetitively using these gestures makes audience engagement falter. Not only are most of them restricting your air, they don't correlate with what you're saying. Add repetition to the mix and they wreck any hope of a fluid journey.

The rule of three

The general rule of gestures in non-verbal studies is that more than two of the same gestures in a row is too much. In music the same principles apply. When you learn composition, the classical form that developed from Handel to Haydn, it follows rules. And one of the rules is you can't repeat something more than twice. You hear it in William Tell for example: dadlum, dadlum, dadlumpumpum. The third time it varies. Same with gestures: do it once, do it twice, don't do it three times in a row. You've lost 'em. These are the triggers.

So: recognise what your gesture pattern is and change it. Change it to a repertoire of gestures that reinforces what you want to say, and on a scale – arms long, wide and high – that has you moving, frees your breathing and guides your air.

The use of gesture was well understood by the Ancient Romans. Their leaders had to try to inspire hordes of citizens to do their bidding, and there were no microphones. These days everyone thinks they need a mic.

I recently worked with an executive to improve his vocal delivery and he said, 'I'm always mic'd up.' And I said, 'How many people are you usually presenting to?' He said, 'Oh, six or seven.' Right, well the Romans didn't have amplifiers as we know them, and leaders presented to tens of thousands of citizens. For the benefit of the plebs at the back, they had heralds stationed on platforms in the crowd at the 150-metre mark who relayed the messages of the orators to people who couldn't hear them directly. But everyone could see and because everybody understood the language of those gestures – because they were congruent with the words they used to reinforce – the influence of these leaders could reach the very back of a stadium or forum, no worries.

Knowledge is power

Although there are no lists of accepted gestures that I know of, here are some general concepts for gestures, some gestures that are widely understood, and a list that shows you how you might create some of your own congruent gestures.

General concepts

Visual concepts are commonly expressed with your hands up high and in front of you, spreading the image out before the audience. You might be saying something like: 'Picture a landscape unmarred by electricity wires.' Hands go up, palms forward. It all hangs together, doesn't it?

Auditory concepts make sense when you use your hands coming in or out wide from either side of your head, at the level of your ears. 'I was listening.' One hand is curved to the side of one ear. 'I'd really value your feedback.' Three fingers draw words from out wide of your ear, inwards.

Kinaesthetic concepts are expressed by hands moving lower. 'I feel' might be hands turned into your lower belly. 'The link between these two ideas' might be hands coming from out wide into fingers linked, one hand into the other.

Widely understood gestures

The future – right hand and arm moving forward and up and a diagonal to your body (your eyes follow your hand).

The past – your left hand throws the past over your left shoulder, gesturing back behind your ear (your eyes straight ahead).
The present – both hands in front, gesturing down crisply to the floor.
Lessons from the past, or a wealth of experience – an imaginary suitcase held to your side, arm bent beside you.
Numbers from one to five – easily expressed with the fingers of one hand held up beside your ear, with your hand turned so the audience can clearly see the number of fingers you're holding up. More than five, you can shake your hand. Numbers gestured like this are very clear – there's little visual distraction.
Excitement – rub your hands together in front of your body.

Holding gestures for congruence

Practise gestures in everyday communications with friends, colleagues, family – even dogs are really into gestures. And practise holding each gesture until you finish the accompanying thought or sentence. That is, don't just flash a number two at the beginning of a sentence such as: 'The two most important aspects of this kind of aeroderivative engine are . . . ' You have to hold the gesture until you finish the sentence, or thought, otherwise the audience can lose the connection. Bringing down the hand or dissolving the gesture indicates the thought is complete.

The no-go zone

Your shoulders and groin form a triangle within which you should try not to gesture. Think of it as the Bermuda Triangle. Don't go there. Gestures in that area convey messages about tension in the body. Also, gestures made close to the body tend to constrict your diaphragm. We want to keep our arms free and clear of the torso when we speak, to encourage both clarity of gesture and our air flow.

And although some gestures do work best in front of your body, it will help your air flow and the visibility of these gestures if you hold them some distance away from your body; don't keep them close and tight.

For obvious reasons, you should also try to avoid gestures that block your face. That is, you want to maintain eye contact with the audience.

The phallic imperative

The other thing about gesturing that uses your fingers is that they have phallic relevance, so they must be erect (settle down, boys at the back). Tony Abbott will say something like, 'There's just one important thing we have to do,' and he'll gesture 'one' with a drooping finger. That's not one important thing. That's a thing that's less and less important as time goes by.

The other thing you're never allowed to do is point – it's way too aggressive. But you can gesture toward someone with a whole, open hand. And you would use an open-hand gesture to ask someone to come up to the stage: 'Would you like to come up to the stage?' Or you might gesture to someone directly to emphasise a point: 'If you want a change of party, you're going to have to vote.' It's not rocket science. But it does take practice.

Arms off (away from your ribs)

So, you're standing front and centre, facing the audience and you say . . . Well, most people come on stage, stand with their arms by their sides, or get behind a lectern, and say, 'Hi, it's really great to be here.'

That's not great! Arms wide is great! One arm high is great! We all imagine that we gesture too flamboyantly, but in fact our gestures usually aren't expressive enough. Our gestures are usually funny, fluttery, habitual things that don't mean anything and that frequently clash with what's coming out of our mouths. Keep in mind that your gestures must be congruent with what you're saying. And if you're using a word such as 'GREAT!', make your gesture congruent. Make it expansive, big and generous.

Try it! Get up. Take the floor. Stand with feet hip-width apart and parallel, knees soft, pelvis tipped under, upper back coming through. Now say your hello with your arms wide and hold that gesture, 'Hello, I'm Louise and it's GREAT TO BE HERE!' Hold your arms up, arms up, arms up. Great! That's it.

Do you feel silly and exposed with your elbows high and your hands higher still? You don't look silly. You look right! Your messages are in concert. It's GREAT to be here. You may think, as I do, that 'It's great to be here!' has become a bit hackneyed, and that people no longer hear it as true, but my point is that even if your greeting is 'Hello! Welcome everyone! I'm Louise,' or whatever it is, say it with conviction and with arms moving off the body and then maintaining that generous embracing movement.

By getting your arms away from your diaphragm you've allowed yourself to breathe freely. The air rushes in, and you're released.

Consider how much more movement we've brought into your presentations. Your diaphragm, your mouth, your eyes, your whole body, your use of the stage and your use of gesture. You now know how to remove the veils on each of them, to release the blockages to flowing breath, thought and voice.

Following is a summary of these three chapters. And make sure you practise. The difference between knowing what to do and applying it is . . . applying it.

Remember, the amateur practises until they get it right. The professional practises until they can't get it wrong.

IN A FEW WORDS

- If someone says you gesture too much or too wildly, it's likely your gestures are simply incongruent. Practise congruent gestures.

- Gestures help you express yourself.

- Gestures reinforce your message to the audience.

- Gestures keep your body moving and your breath flowing – in fact, they guide your breath.

- Avoid incongruent, laughable gestures.

- Twice is enough when it comes to consecutive gestures.

- Practice congruent, message-reinforcing gestures.

- Visual concepts are gestured high, in front of you, above your head with the palms of your hands out.

- Auditory concepts are gestured on either side of your head – at ear level.

- Kinaesthetic concepts are gestured low with palms facing in.

- Hold a congruent gesture until the thought or sentence is complete.

- Straighten up those phallic gestures; don't go limp.

- Incorporate a big arm movement into your introduction. 'Welcome! It's great to see you all here, I'm Louise Mahler!' and raise your arms away from your sides in a welcoming gesture.

No sex with the props!

One important thing about whiteboards, blackboards, easels of butcher's paper and PowerPoints. You never want to be turned towards and talking to the visuals. Do not abandon your audience for your prepared materials. Again, it's a breaking of contact, the ruination of trust, and an invitation for people to start downloading a game on their iPhone, or to check their texts.

Using whiteboards requires you to co-ordinate your eyes, gestures and movement. You touch the whiteboard at the point you're about to refer to – and yes, you can look at the whiteboard as you touch it (the audience knows what you're looking at and they are also following your gaze) – then you turn back to the audience to explain the point. You stop talking. Indicate your next point on the whiteboard or PowerPoint. Turn back to the audience. Explain.

PART THREE

Putting it all together

IN EMERGENCY, BREAK GLASS: THE EXPRESS PATH TO VOCAL INTELLIGENCE

Seriously? You skipped straight to this chapter?

Ah, so you're someone who likes a quick fix? I'm sorry, but there just isn't one for what we're doing. There's real work, learning and self-reflection involved in this process.

Progress is a pretty straightforward model for change, and no-one else can do your homework for you. So, unless you want to resort to alcohol and drugs (it's true, they *can* deliver a temporary fix for public-speaking nerves, if that's all you're after), flick right back to the first chapter and let's do this thing.

Or, if you're still standing in the bookshop and this all sounds too hard, just put me back on the shelf – you're not ready to change yet. See you when you are!

Love, Louise x

IN EMERGENCY, BREAK GLASS: THE EXPRESS PATH TO VOCAL INTELLIGENCE

PERFORMANCE ANXIETY

So, we've done the dance of the seven veils. A little bit of news, though. I have to tell you that even though you now know how to lift all your veils, they're always going to be wafting about. You have the tools to fold them away, but this chapter will serve as a reminder that even when you've got it nailed (and even when it's your life's work, as it is for me), you can't afford to be smug. Pride comes before a false vocal fold!

I've had performance anxiety all my life. I'm living proof that knowing the tricks and triggers doesn't mean the end of fight or flight. However, you can learn to control it.

Studies show that the worst cases of performance anxiety start at around five or six years old – that's the earliest you can get it. The later it sets in, the easier it can be to overcome. Before that we're happily bouncing around, showing off, doing our thing, thinking everyone loves us. It's always some trauma that triggers it, even if it seems to be minor. The longer you've been living with that trigger, the harder the anxiety is to cure. The interesting thing about people who have performance anxiety is that often they'll keep throwing themselves into performance situations to try to cure it, but they usually throw themselves in with no solutions except hope. (I remind you, you now have hope *and* a brand new skill set!)

It is common for me to meet people who believe they just need to 'relax' and be themselves. This was what a senior business leader said to me recently before being thrown to the radio wolves to defend his company's latest decision. Two things come to mind when I hear this. Firstly, what exactly is relaxing about sitting opposite a shock-jock who's trying to eat you for breakfast? Secondly, what do you mean by 'being yourself'? If you don't know your responses under stress, you don't know which fraction of yourself is going to turn up. It is more than likely going to be one tiny piece of who you are, sitting there in crisis, with one-tenth of the oxygen you need to think, and one-200th of your emotional capacity transformed into sound.

I've had difficult experiences many, many times. Throughout my career in the opera, I fought my performance anxiety on a daily basis. I remember it clearly: there I was, with the Vienna State Opera, feeling really sick with chronic bronchitis (Mimi!). My vocal folds were swollen and we had a big show coming up. We were doing a rehearsal and all the important people were there to see us – we were all the young stars. I got up to sing and *nothing* came out. I cried: 'I'm sick! I'm sick!' And I got on a plane and left. I went to England. I got into terrible trouble, because I was under contract, of course. I had no right to just up and leave. But I kept protesting: 'I'm sick! I'm sick!' I *was* sick, but that illness was exacerbated by performance anxiety.

This was before I'd worked on my body jams with Professor Müller-Preis. Her work helped me hugely, because they had never been dealt with before. Ultimately, I was shown how to clear them, and then I became more interested in those jams than in singing, which is how I came to be doing what I'm doing today.

It is years since I had a bout of performance anxiety. But the truth is, it can take you by surprise. On the last occasion, I was tired. The audience were not who I thought they would be. Nothing was as I had imagined it. I was fine with it and then suddenly a voice behind me said, 'You are going to be good, aren't you?' For some reason that set off an old response.

Performance anxiety is different for everyone. Some people cannot sleep for three months before an engagement. For many it comes on at the final moments. My experience is just before a performance, as though time is frozen. Sound comes out, but the thinking is blurred. I experience a disconnect. I am talking more to myself than those around me. And then, when the show is over and I wake up at 3 a.m., as I did the following night on this occasion, I find myself sitting bolt upright and saying, 'Oh God, I didn't finish that sentence.' This is known as rumination.

What happened to me that time was not so much a crisis, but it was definitely *ordinary*. The fascinating thing is that some people didn't even notice. Performance anxiety is like that. It is hard to convince someone who has these experiences that resolving them is not always for the audience's sake. Overcoming your anxiety can be about your own comfort.

On another occasion, many years ago, the finals of the Australian Singing Competition were being held at the Sydney Opera House. I walked on stage and there, five metres in front of me, was my idol, Dame Joan Sutherland, staring straight at me. In retrospect, I could have reframed my fear as a great honour and risen to the occasion, but I remember it as a nightmare of performance anxiety and tortured myself about it for decades. Quite recently, the videos of those performances were released on YouTube. I watched them and lo and behold, my performance was not nearly as bad as I'd imagined.

One learns that nothing is ever as bad as you think (and correspondingly, unfortunately, no performance is ever as good as you might think.)

I know the tricks. I'm the one telling other people how to unblock. So what went wrong on that occasion? The important thing is to focus and refocus on learning, learning and more learning. So, I searched for something I could learn – and this time it was something about my psychological triggers.

When I was young, I used to do ballet and theatre and whatever silliness my mother thought was a brilliant idea (with whatever psychopath was conducting those sessions in pre-modern suburban BrisVegas). If you remember, she had this unfulfilled desire to be a singer herself. She translated this into ambition for me, and I was put into *everything*. I was too big for ballet: I was tall and ballet dancers are traditionally expected to be petite. I left the Brownies when I had to dance round a mushroom singing, 'We're the tweenies short and small. We'll be Brownies when we are tall.'

And at my all-girls' school, I always seemed to end up playing a German soldier in the school play, so it was hardly what I would call rewarding theatre. I performed all through my childhood and every single time, before I'd go on, my mother would say to me, very intensely: 'You're going to be good for Mummy, aren't you?' I've realised it's that phrase that triggers me. It's not 'Be good for the audience', and it's not 'Be good for yourself.' It's not 'Have fun!' No, it's 'Be good for *Mummy!*' And if you analyse that – which I have, obviously – it's an unachievable goal. So I never achieved it; it was a lose-lose proposition.

And so the minute I go into a performance where I have to 'Be good for someone', that's my trigger. It's no longer about the material, it's no longer about entertainment, it's not about enjoyment – it's just about someone who exists to be impressed. It's my trigger.

I had never really articulated it in that way before, and a trigger recognised is an evil you can fight and overcome.

An old actor's adage is: 'How do you get over nerves? You don't. You learn how to deal with them.'

So here's the other thing I have to tell you: you're *never* completely cured. You're always going to have your triggers, and sometimes they'll shoot you right in the throat. The only thing you can do is keep practising all your skills, so you know what to do to unblock, and to be aware of your triggers. Awareness is the remedy.

Performance anxiety and social anxiety are different things

We used to think that performance anxiety was linked to social anxiety – that if you couldn't perform, it was because you had some broader psychological issue. But we now know that's not true.

159

Performance anxiety does not have to be part and parcel with other social phobias, even when it comes on suddenly and stops a previously confident speaker in their tracks with such force that you think there's something huge going on in their minds. There *is*, but they might not suffer from other types of anxiety.

I had a client who was a super salesman – totally confident and used to giving big presentations, really at the top of his game. And then one day, he was asked a question he didn't have the answer for, and he just froze.

So we talked. And the whole theme of everything he was telling me was uncertainty. We were just talking about work, where nothing had really changed, but his uncertainty was palpable. So I kept him talking around that theme, pulling on that thread with him. And eventually he told me that his wife had recently been diagnosed with cancer, had undergone surgery and was now doing chemotherapy.

Talk about stress and uncertainty! This poor guy – he hadn't even realised how deeply it was affecting him. He was, naturally, really anxious about his wife and what was happening to her, and that awful uncertainty had really gripped his psyche without him knowing it. It led to his panic onstage when he was asked a question when previously, even if he hadn't had the exact answer, he would have been able to glide over it with ease. He didn't see the connection between the serious uncertainty in his personal life and how it was affecting his professional life.

Uncertainty was his trigger, and once he knew that, he could look out for it. He understood that was why he sometimes felt that way during a presentation, and he could deal with it. And I'm so pleased to be able to tell you that his wife was pronounced cancer-free at the end of her treatment.

Tiredness

It's also important to be conscious of tiredness. It's crazy, but people don't respect how tiredness affects their voices. Remember, voice is a physical force. You wouldn't go and run a half-marathon if you were exhausted, so of course you can't do a presentation on three hours of sleep.

There's no cure for tiredness other than rest. This is why professional singers swaddle themselves in cotton wool. It's 'Quiet, don't disturb Pavarotti!' They have guards around the dressing rooms. Singers won't talk for the whole day before a big performance. They rest. Because if you're tired and your vocal folds are tired, they just don't work and there's nothing you can do to fix it. (Not to mention how tiredness affects your capacity to think!)

Tiredness is one thing. Vocal damage is another. My work is with psychologically sound, healthy professionals who have a need to engage. The voice as a transformation of personal energy into sound is just that; we are not battling with physical swelling from abuse. If you do have a physical problem, it's best to see an ear, nose and throat specialist.

The curse of video

Here's another thing I counsel against: videoing as a way of training. Many presentation coaches do this and while it might work for some, I question the results. As singers we *never, ever, ever* used video, and I can't say I have ever seen it in theatre. So why, then, is video so often the medium of choice for corporate change?

There are two things against it: acoustics and psychology. When you're speaking, singing and hearing yourself, what you hear most easily is the resonance inside your head. You also hear some of your own sound as it comes back to you, but when it does, you get more of the lower frequencies than the higher ones. So we hear what's in our head, and we hear the lower frequencies of our sound bouncing back to us. What we hear of ourselves is richer and warmer than what others hear when we speak.

My point about any recording of yourself for the purposes of training is that it's deceptive. It's an acoustic challenge. Yes, you sound different, but that's because you're hearing it in a completely different form when you're playing it back to yourself. In my view, it's like the whole perception palaver in non-verbal studies. It's interesting, but it won't help you work out what you need to change.

And here's the other thing to be aware of, if someone tries to talk you into such a recording of yourself: it can be too painful to hear what you sound like. There's too much pain in watching yourself. Sure, there will be times when we have to hear or watch ourselves played back: a speech at a wedding, a radio interview, perhaps even a presentation you've given that's been recorded by your company. I'm just saying, beware.

Most often, a more effective vehicle for change is to consider the immediacy of feedback from a trusted advisor in the moment. Masterclasses are the go!

That is because voice is a kinaesthetic experience. You are (or you should be) feeling your voice more than you are hearing it. I know that sounds weird, but your aim is to get the sensation of *resonance* in your voice. As long as you keep practising the skills we've learned through this book, you'll be constantly putting yourself on the path to resonance. Becoming aware of your body's twists and turns can be a good indication of unnecessary tension.

Once you get your vocal intelligence humming, you will be able to isolate your own resonance. You can feel it under your eyes, you feel no tension, you engage the lower body, and you go, 'Ahhhhhh'. That's when you know your sound is flowing.

Singers often have factors such as a large orchestra that stops them from hearing themselves, but you can feel the production of sound. You embody the sound so that you resonate.

Once you have begun on your path to resonance, you're doing a lot of things that will help you avoid performance anxiety, because you've made the good habits your new pattern and you feel unhindered and unblocked.

There are a couple more pieces of knowledge that will help you along the way.

Find your frequency

Here's a cold hard fact: if you're a woman, your voice is an octave higher than a man's. And the challenge for women is that culturally we associate low, slow and loud voices with authority – to us, that's the voice of leadership. It's why men can get away with so much, thanks to their naturally deeper sound. It is so unfair that men can have people in the palm of their hands simply because their voices are deep and loud. As a consequence, they are believed to be confident and strong.

The obvious message is that if you want to be a leader, you should use a voice that's low, slow and loud. But if you're a woman, you can't. Your voice may not only be a full octave higher, but, due to the smaller size of your vocal mechanism, it will have less volume. And if that's you, if you try to alter it, you'll sound fake. Coming across as inauthentic is way worse. You lose people a lot faster if you don't sound genuine.

The other thing to know is that everyone has a 'fundamental frequency'. This is the pitch at which your voice sits at its most comfortable. Fundamental frequency is your voice's natural home, if you like. It's determined by the shape of your throat, so you really can't change it.

To find yours, try making this sound:
Ommmmmmmmmmmmmmmmmmmmmmmmmmmmmm.

That sound – wherever you land when you do that without forcing anything – is your fundamental frequency.

So while some may encourage women with high-pitched voices to pitch lower, I'm telling you: no. Work on your veils, unblock yourself, unleash your natural, authentic voice – I promise it will work for you. We have to work smarter, not harder.

Where movement and mantra meet

As a little aside, here's one engagement strategy. To be honest, it's a method of self-distraction I use before presenting to big groups of people of whom I am uncertain.

At the Australian Human Resources Institute conference one year, there were 1500 people, all HR managers. In this kind of situation, my reputation is either made or broken right there and then – I'm only as good as my last performance. It's vital for me to start with confidence. So before people went into the room I moved around among them, talking to as many of them as I could: 'Hi, my name's Louise, what are you hoping to get out of today?', 'What do you do?', 'Where do you come from?', 'What is the key thing you have learnt today so far?'. I connected with as many people as possible. And now I had a 'friend group' before I went onstage.

When the announcer said ' . . . and welcome Dr Louise Mahler!', my mind said, 'We're on, friends!' And as I was going up the stairs, I was looking out at all the friends I'd made. There were all these voices in my head going, 'But this could *kill* you. Maybe you'll be terrible,' or whatever. But I brushed those negative voices off in favour of a mantra I repeated silently to the audience: 'I love you, I love you, I love you.'

Ruby Wax has also mentioned using this as her strategy. I do not imagine the audience in the nude, or mentally put them in a box. I cannot.

If I don't get the chance to meet and greet people, I use a similar connecting mantra. I find a place where I can look at the assembled group before it's my time to speak, and I find people's faces in the crowd and I think, 'I love you.

I love you. I love you.'

It's got to be the right mantra. It can't be, 'It's going to be good. It's going to be good,' because your unconscious mind might say, 'Well, it wasn't last time!' It has to be an indisputable mantra. 'I love you' works because it reminds your subconscious that you're here for a reason, to deliver a message, whatever it is, that will allow the audience to achieve something or understand something they didn't know before. It reminds you that you are there with a purpose: to benefit this group.

TRICKS OF THE TRADE

So, friends, we've come to the end of the book – and to the beginning of your life as a master of vocal intelligence. I want to leave you with a grab-bag of tricks, tips, tools and trigger warnings. By now you'll know which of these you need most, and which parts of this book you'll need to dip back into from time to time. Remember, practise, practise, practise (but make sure you are practising the right things!).

Also, remember your mind-body-voice spiral, and that you can train your rational mind to be the boss of that wonderful whirlpool. And promise me that you will forever remember that your voice, a physical force, is as much about your body as it is about your breath.

10 PRINCIPLES OF VOCAL INTELLIGENCE

1. Each person is born with a perfect instrument.
2. It gives you an enormous range and flexibility of sound.
3. All people can sing.
4. There are no bad sounds.
5. There are unhealthy sounds.
6. Voice is released, not taught.
7. We can release it at any age.
8. Vocal dynamics echo psychodynamics.
9. The voice is the mind reflected through the body.
10. There is no personal change without vocal change and vice versa – there is no vocal change without personal change.

Let's go over some of the ground we've covered, so you can start putting all you've learned into practice.

Practising in the mirror will only get you so far

The principles of practice are that you can't only do it before the mirror or in the bathroom. Anyone can sing in the shower, or practise in the safety of their own bedroom. Do it by all means, but you'll need to take it further. It's *context* that counts. By practising with people, you will steadily embed your learning into your unconscious. You can do your 'Hi, hi, hi' exercise with your kids, or do it when you're driving and pretend you're talking to the people in the other cars. You can do it with your dog. The unconscious mind needs the smell, feel and vibration of living beings around you. It needs context.

So go in with purpose when you give your favourite barista your morning coffee order. 'Hi, hi, hi! Can I have a strong latte?' Get your voice resonating all the way to the coffee beans.

Some more secrets to help you nail your presentation

Whether you're preparing to give a talk in a boardroom or ball-room, try to get into the physical space ahead of time to rehearse and plot your moves. I can't overstate how important this is.

For the boardroom, it's figuring out where you'll be stand-ing or sitting. Working out the height of the table, the height of the chair, what the acoustics of the room feel like, so that you're totally comfortable on the day. And for the ballroom, it's actually counting out the number of steps from offstage or where you'll be seated waiting to go on, to the lectern or the centre of the stage, where you'll begin your presentation.

I always arrive the night before a big gig and if it's in a hotel, I'll stay in that hotel and ask to see the room that's going to be used for the event the next day. They'll say, 'Oh, but it's not set up.' I don't care. I need to see the size of the room. I need to see where the vibrations are going to go when I speak. I need to feel out my steps and plot the stage out for myself. I need to see and feel the perspective.

And when you come to the point where you're about to take the stage for your presentation, I'm going to assume that you've got all seven veils folded away neatly in their box and you're ready to rock your vocal intelligence. These tips are about stagecraft.

First, the run-and-stop entrance. It definitely requires some confidence to pull it off, but it's a great way to both prepare yourself and attract attention.

It pumps up the energy in the room when the MC says, 'And now we'd like to welcome Louise Mahler to the stage.' It's imperative that you know where you are on the line-up, that you are literally on the edge of your seat (with your power at the ready in your lower body) and ready to stand as they start introducing you, especially if you're coming from a seat in the audience or elsewhere on the stage. If you're in the wings, just be there, have that diaphragm unjammed (cough if you need to, to kickstart it) and be ready to trot out onstage the second he or she says your name. Feel the energy. When they are finished applauding your introduction, you are on.

You enter purposefully, without speaking – that's important – and you stop. A lot of magicians use this to attract attention for their acts – all sorts of performers do. Some actually run on, but if that's not your style, at least move with purpose and then stop. You'll find that this go-stop entrance also changes your voice; it gives it a deeper timbre because your body has had that little burst of movement and is primed for action. It really works. Give it a go-stop! Run, stop. 'Hello everyone, I'm Louise and today I'm going to give you all the keys to vocal intelligence.'

If you're in a boardroom situation, all sitting around, often the introduction you get is very lazy and casual. 'OK, Louise, what have you got to say?' And if you're sitting back, or have your legs crossed, or you're hunched over, you can't begin talking from any of those positions – you haven't set up your instrument. It's fine if you're sitting back when they do their laidback throw to your part of the meeting. But as soon as they do, move to the front of your chair, sit forward, put your hands on the table and begin. In fact, even if you are already sitting up, make sure you make a move; make a change to signify you're on. Don't start speaking until you're in position. It's the boardroom table version of go-stop and it brings your act together.

You learned about the rest position in the chapter on posture, and also the use of gestures, as well as tips on eye movement – all great presentation skills, but also great for helping you unblock. If you're speaking on your feet, you'll want to choose different physical spaces for the different parts of your engagement too. This applies whether you're on a stage, in a less formal conference room or even at a table in a meeting. It helps to embed your messages with them, but more importantly it helps you breathe, to move, to be free.

If you're in a boardroom, you probably won't be able to move around much, but if it's possible, find a way to be on your feet to speak. Consider having a prop such as putting a part of your presentation on a whiteboard or flipchart, to make sense of you standing away from the table. And make sure you assume the rest position if you're asking for questions at the end (if you're seated, you can do this by putting one relaxed hand on top of the other). Anything else sends psychological messages that you're not really open to questions, but more importantly, might not set you up for your own sound.

... even if they can't see you

On the phone, your voice becomes even more important because it's speaking for your mind and your body.

In the body-language world of non-verbal studies, voice and body are treated as if they're separate. But vocal intelligence recognises that voice and body are one (with the mind at the centre of the spiral). So just because you're on the phone, you can't let your body go – don't sit down. If it's an important call, treat it like a gig. You've got to stand up, you've got to do all of those things you would do if you were there to impress in person. If possible, use a headset, so that you can be hands-free and use all of the opening-up gestures you would if you were in the room with the person or people on the other end of the phone. Including your body in the act of speaking is essential, even when you're invisible to your audience.

If you're a woman

Despite Helen Reddy's call back in the Seventies – 'I am woman, hear me roar!' – by and large, women still aren't heard. It's a physiological fact that a woman's voice is less powerful and an octave higher than a man's, so what can you do? If you've climbed the Stairway to the Stars in this book, you've already taken leaps and bounds to being heard. These tips are exactly the same for men, but because of the perception of the voice of leadership in Western culture (low, slow and loud) and the intense scrutiny women are subjected to, a woman cannot afford to get it wrong. Here are a few reminders:

- Recognise that stress can take the voice high and that the higher you go, the less relevant and less audible you become. So make sure you listen for it in yourself. Then use your rational mind and your body-unjamming techniques to kick yourself out (see page 56 for a reminder). Return to your fundamental frequency, which will be higher than a man's, but won't be as high as your squeaky stress pitch.

- If you have a visual learning preference, remember this will also take you higher. Learn to help control your voice through your eyes.

- Similarly, avoid the baby voice that women use even when they're not in stressful situations. *Please!* 'What was that, darling? You *do* want to go to the shop?' It's not healthy to speak like a child.

- Avoid the double-jeopardy of baby voice plus upward inflection, where the voice goes up at the end of sentences: 'I think that'd be a really good *idea*.' Also avoid the nasal whine with the upward inflection to close (often heard in shop assistants): 'And how are you *today*?' It's so undermining. You're not helping yourself, you're not helping the world, you're not helping womankind, you're not helping Australia. Pull yourself together; don't do it!

- Remember that the advice of Sheryl Sandberg, COO of Facebook, to 'lean in' is figurative, not literal. When you lean in physically you can go to aggression rather than power; you squeeze the body and voice and diminish your message.

- Don't undermine your credibility with 'vocal fry'.

- Do use the voice of sexual excitement for caring situations. Don't fake it, but recognise if you are tight and strained when you should be hearing some low sounds with escaping air.

- Use your hand gestures rather than head movements to communicate – opting for the latter will squash your sound.

- Find excuses to stand and walk to gain power and free the body.

- Use movement and gestures to describe and strengthen your points, rather than relying on the raw tools of power and depth of sound.

Remember that you now have the skills to deal with an onslaught

Learning how to hold on to your skills in stressful situations is at the heart of vocal intelligence. When you've practised and practised, nothing can rattle you (well, it might, but you'll be able to power through it). Reminding yourself that you are now wielding a powerful voice arsenal will make you feel mighty in any situation.

I remember one client, Jill, who was charged with being the public voice of her organisation. Her role was to embody the warm, caring, conversational front the organisation wanted to convey. But the problem was that the organisation she was representing certainly didn't have a warm, caring or conversational image – so it was a big ask.

Jill herself had these qualities, and a lot of innate skills in public speaking. She was good. But the effort required to maintain her sense of self when she was under stress – such as being badgered in a live interview on radio – on a regular basis, was breaking her down. She had been torn apart in public many times and, understandably, it was taking its toll. She had lost her confidence.

As we talked our way through Jill's role and how she was approaching it, I realised that the very fact that Jill's skills were so inherent was part of her problem. She was a natural and had never consciously unpacked them. So when she was under great stress, which scrambles our natural skills, she didn't know how to reach for them.

Together, we worked on her technique for initiating the engagement with her questioners, techniques for creating a 'holding pattern' and processes for managing every permutation and combination of questioning. Once she knew what she was doing right and added a few more ideas, she knew how to mentally reach for them when she was under fire. She also got in the habit of rehearsing a difficult media interview ahead of time with a colleague whenever possible.

After our final session, Jill wrote to me:
'I want to take this moment to thank you for all the help and support that you've provided me with over the past few months. I say this with all sincerity; there have been very few individuals who have had such a significant impact on my professional life, as you have. Your advice and guidance has certainly helped me to

overcome some of the fear I held regarding the media component of my role, and for that I am extremely thankful. Whilst I found the process at times incredibly challenging and very confronting, I have learned more from you in those short sessions than I have from others whom I have worked with for years.'

Nurture your vocal fitness

If you didn't already, you now know the dire effect tiredness has on your voice and how the only cure for it is rest. But here's a bigger 'Dos and Don'ts' list to remind you of how to look after your vocal health so that it can look after you.

Vocal professionals pretty much nurture their instrument 24/7. You'll break these rules sometimes, but being aware of them will lead you to treat your voice with more respect. (And you'll see so much of it has to do with your *body*.)

- Avoid speaking when ill.
- Avoid alcohol.
- Get ample sleep.
- Make sure you avoid smoke and smokers; stay in smoke-free hotels.
- Drink at least two litres of water a day to keep the body (and throat) hydrated.
- Avoid drastic temperature changes.
- Don't yell (for both your voice and for your sanity!).
- Don't whisper (it strains the vocal folds even more).
- Avoid noisy environments over which you have to speak loudly to be heard.

- Avoid 'glottal attack' (where you crash your vocal folds together, without the breath, most commonly for the vowel sounds 'ah' and 'eh').
- Work on your fitness, breathing and posture.
- Understand your voice.
- Use techniques to keep stress out of the throat.
- Don't clear your throat, swallow instead.

Even if you don't treat yourself like a Pavarotti, if you follow these rules as much as you can, your voice will thank you. Next time you have occasion to yell – say you see a dog running out on to the road and you scream 'STOOOPPPP!' – you'll really notice how much it hurts and how for the next twenty-four hours your voice suffers.

These three associations are all good sources of further information and advice on vocal health: the Australian National Association of Teachers of Singing; the Voice and Speech Trainers Association and the British Voice Association. Google them and have a little explore around their websites.

If you're an asthmatic who needs to use a corticosteroid preventer spray, you probably already know that it has an effect on the vocal folds, possibly giving you a sore throat and even making you hoarse at times. I'm not saying you should stop the spray. But do be aware of the effect it has and follow the directions to minimise those side effects. You may also wish to discuss with your doctor whether drugs with finer particles, which leave less residue of the medication in the throat, might be suitable for you.

Consider having some professional coaching

That sounds like a blatant pitch for business, but it's not really. I'm only one person out here and as much as I'd love to, I probably can't get to you all!

But now that you've done all of the work in this book to hone your vocal intelligence, having a session or two with a professional coach would be the icing on the cake. Make sure you find someone with good credentials, for example someone who is a working public speaker themselves, or if you're interested in working on your singing voice, someone who's been a professional singer. You want to find someone who's going to listen and watch your style carefully so they can help you build on your strengths and pack away your weaknesses.

Of course, I do offer retreats, as well as corporate mentoring sessions, and I'd love to have you along, especially as you would be coming so well primed. If you're interested, you'll find details (as well as a lot more information, and my blog) on my website: www.louisemahler.com.au. And here endeth the plug!

Time to say goodbye

I hate goodbyes, so I've added a postscript chapter, written by one of the wonderful people I studied and worked with for my PhD. I truly hope you have enjoyed the journey on which this book has taken you, and that the skills you've learned will stay with you for life. (Remember: practise!)

Karen is absolutely fabulous, so I'm going to give her the final word.

POSTSCRIPT: KAREN'S STORY

Karen was one of the generous people who agreed to join me in my PhD research. We worked together for over a year – Karen even had some confronting, amazing sessions with Professor Müller-Preis. At the end, she wrote this about the process we'd followed:

'My friend Tricia asked me if I would like to join her and be a subject in a PhD study on voice, and that's how I met Louise. I'd often thought about having some coaching to improve my voice. I had a crap voice, in my opinion. I couldn't be heard – I just wasn't loud enough. I couldn't project my voice and even if I could, it sounded awful: small, high, thin. A voice with not a lot of substance or authority. A crap voice was not a good look in my field of work. I'm a consultant in organisational development and I facilitate a lot of groups and workshops.

'I had been paying a lot of attention to "finding my own voice", metaphorically speaking – discovering and expressing

179

myself. Tricia's invitation seemed timely; it seemed natural to continue by literally finding my voice. So I was instantly alert, and a little afraid, as I plunged into this unexpected opportunity.

'I was very apprehensive as I went to meet Louise. I didn't know what to expect or how it would work. Louise swept in, a wave of energy and enthusiasm, that told me I was on the right track. And so the voice work began.

'We met one-on-one every week or so for an hour or more. I had no idea about the physiology of voice, of how sound happened. I wanted to develop a clear, strong and commanding voice. One that had authority and substance; that expressed groundedness and presence.

'Very quickly, I realised just how constrained I felt. I often felt inhibited. Some of the exercises with Louise were confronting. I was often self-conscious. Over time, I came to see how many strictures and plain old unhelpful beliefs were getting in my way. I thought I was one of those people who had been born with a terrible voice. It was genetic. There was nothing I could do about it, except shout every now and then.

'I hadn't sung much after fifth-grade choir – which I had loved, and thought I was pretty good at. I don't really understand why that changed. Somewhere along the line, I came to believe I had an awful sound. I think I was told I did, and assumed it was true. A self-fulfilling prophecy was set in motion. That's why I stopped singing out loud or in front of others. I was too embarrassed to expose myself in that way. And anyway, being loud was just plain rude. My work with Louise slowly uncovered just how many knots I had tied my voice up in.

'Louise talked about a process for increasing my vocal intelligence. I had to unlearn much of what I was habitually doing.

It had a lot to do with repetition and practice, practice, practice. I learned that breathing, speaking and singing are all the same basic function: if you can do one, you can do them all. It's a very positive, encouraging and freeing approach. These are all words that absolutely describe Louise and the process we were engaged in.

'I learned so many different things about how to fully inhabit my voice and my body. I felt a lot of anxiety. Over time, this has certainly diminished, but in the early stages, being a learner was accompanied by the vulnerability of uncertainty and doubt. I was learning a new language with many technical terms that describe sound. Many times I did not understand what was being asked of me.

'Louise responded by building bridges from one language to the other. She used many metaphors and visual images to express herself and this helped me enormously. I could quickly connect with what was being asked of me. I could, in fact, get it. Yippee!

'She'd say: "It's like biting the apple – just pretend you are biting the apple when you sing this note!" Bang – I got it. My mouth assumed the position and the note just followed, clear and right where it needed to be. I love that experience, when you struggle, struggle, struggle and then it all comes together in the moment. Learning new postures and positions, learning technique was challenging, confronting, exhilarating and intense.

'I really noticed the results when I was running the first workshop of a new program for about ninety people: big in size and occasion. As I moved around the room I noticed my feet were firm on the ground. My legs were strong. When I moved or stood, I was tall and straight, balanced, grounded. We were using microphones, but at some point during the day I was asked to speak without a mic. I stood up, opened my mouth and spoke. I knew I was loud because I could hear my voice coming back at me from the other side of the room. It was a very big room. I was gobsmacked! How's that for feedback?

'I have a voice.

'The sessions with Louise continued, using different exercises to strengthen or clarify technique or sound, and learning more and more about breathing. In the early sessions, I constantly felt like I was running out of breath. Louise said something very interesting: rather than running out of breath, I was running into resistance. Somehow that very different spin helped. With practice, my breathing developed. I feel as if I have bellows inside of me now; my breath moving in and out feels exactly how I imagine bellows to be.

'That curiosity, that partnership has led me on a journey where I'm doing a lot of rearranging and reorienting of my identity towards Karen with a Voice, Karen Who Can Learn and Sing a Song, Karen Who Can Be Heard.

'So where am I now?

'I project my voice more readily now. I have increased the volume, and can increase it even more if I need to. I have much more confidence in my voice. I also know a lot more about what gets in my way, physically and emotionally.

'I listen to voices differently. I hear things I didn't hear before. I pay attention and observe how others make sound. I'm fascinated by singers in particular. My appreciation of singing has deepened.

'I stand more firmly on the ground. I have greater balance.

I am less challenged by heights and can climb more readily up and down ladders, for example. I feel more grounded. I continue with the exercises; they are part of my daily routine. My bowleggedness has diminished. My posture has improved enormously. My physical capacities and body awareness continue to develop.

'I am even more strongly committed to practice, practice, practice. The willingness to be a learner is a fundamental life skill. Curiosity and partnership are essential ingredients. What a blessing to find Louise.'

ACKNOWLEDGEMENTS

To the participants and leaders on whom,
let's face it, I learnt my trade. Thank you.
I would like to thank my patient husband, Hermann,
and my children Oliver and Colette. Good work team!
So many strong mentors shine through: Dame Elizabeth
Schwarzkopf, Professor Müeller-Preis, Sir Peter Pears and
Peter Ustinov. And my thanks to Natalie Filatoff and Jane Nicholls,
who helped me find the right words. I would have to spare a place,
too, for my horse, Sir James, who, like Mr Ed, has listened to every
step along the way. He has been very obliging.

Throughout the book, I have given some case studies based
on work I've done with people. They are composites and
names have been changed to protect their privacy.

BIBLIOGRAPHY

Abram, D. (1996). *The Spell of the Sensuous: Perception and Language in a More-than-human World*. New York, Pantheon Books.

Alexander, F. M. (1985). *The Use of the Self*. London, Victor Gollancz Limited.

Barton, R. (1997). 'Voice in a Visual World' in *The Vocal Vision*. M. Hampton and B. Acker. New York, Applause Books: 81–92.

Berry, C. (1973). *Voice and the Actor*. New York, Macmillan.

Berry, C. (1975). *Your Voice and How to Use It Successfully*. London, Harrap Limited.

Berry, C. (1997). 'That Secret Voice' in *The Vocal Vision*. M. Hampton and B. Acker. New York, Applause Books: 25–35.

Davis, P. (1998). 'Emotional Influences on Singing' in *Australian Voice* 4: 13–18.

Estill, J. (1997). *Compulsory Figures for Voice: A user's guide to voice quality: Level One – Primer of Basic Figures*. Santa Rosa, Estill Voice Training Systems.

Feldenkrais, D. M. (1981). *The Elusive Obvious*. Capitola, CA, Meta Publications.

Hampton, M. and B. Acker, Eds. (1997). *The Vocal Vision: Views on Voice*. New York, London, Applause.

Handel, S. (1991). *Listening: An introduction to the perception of auditory events*. London, The MIT Press.

Kittelson, M. L. (1996). *Sounding the Soul: The Art of Listening*. Einsiedeln, Switzerland, Daimon.

Lessac, A. (1997). *The Use and Training of the Human Voice*. London, Mayfield Publishing Company.

Linklater, K. (1976). *Freeing the Natural Voice*. New York, Drama Book Publishers.

Linklater, K. (1997). 'Thoughts on theatre, therapy and the art of voice' in *The Vocal Vision: Views on Voice*. M. Hampton and B. Acker. New York, Applause Books: 3–12.

Litante, J. (1962). *A Natural Approach to Singing*. London, Oxford University Press.

Locke, J. L. (1998). *The Devoicing of Society: Why We Don't Talk to Each Other Any More*. New York, Simon & Schuster.

Meigs, M. M. (1994). 'Therapeutic Voicework' in *Innovative Therapy: A Handbook*. D. Jones. Buckingham, Open University Press: 174–188.

Moses, P. J. (1954). *The Voice of Neurosis*. New York, Grune & Stratton.

Moustakas, C. (1990). *Heuristic Research: Design, Methodology, and Applications*. London, Sage Publications.

BIBLIOGRAPHY

Nelson, S. H. and E. Blades-Zeller (2002). *Singing with your Whole Self: The Feldenkrais Method and Voice*. London, The Scarecrow Press Inc.

Newham, P. (1990). 'The Voice and the Shadow' in *Performance* 60: 38–47.

Newham, P. (1992). 'Jung and Alfred Wolfsohn: Analytical psychology and the singing voice' in *Journal of Analytical Psychology* 37: 323–336.

Newham, P. (1993). 'The psychology of voice and the founding of the Roy Hart Theatre' in *New Theatre Quarterly* 33: 59–65.

Newham, P. (1997). *The Prophet of Song: The life and work of Alfred Wolfsohn*. London, Tigers Eye Press.

Newham, P. (1998). *Therapeutic Voicework – Principles and Practice for the Use of Singing as a Therapy*. London, Jessica Kingsley Publishers.

Newham, P. (1999a). *The Healing Voice*. Melbourne, Victoria, Element.

Newham, P. (1999b). *Using Voice and Song in Therapy*. London, Jessica Kingsley Publishers.

Newham, P. (1999c). *Using Voice and Movement in Therapy*. London, Jessica Kingsley Publishers.

Newham, P. (2000). *Using Voice and Theatre in Therapy*. London, Jessica Kingsley Publishers.

Rodenburg, P. (1992). *The Right to Speak*. New York, Routledge.

Rodenburg, P. (1997). 'Re-discovering lost voices' in *The Vocal Vision*. M. Hampton and B. Acker. New York, Applause Books: 37–41.

Rodenburg, P. (1997). *The Actor Speaks*. New York, St Martin's Press.

Rosen, D. and R. Sataloff (1997). *Psychology of Voice Disorders*. London, Singular Publishing Group.

Sataloff, R. T., Ed. (1998). *Voice Perspectives*. San Diego, Singular Publishing.

Stark, J. (1999). *Bel canto: A History of Vocal Pedagogy*. Toronto, University of Toronto Press.

Steiner, R. (1964). *The Arts and their Mission*. New York, Anthroposophic Press.

Stengel, I. and T. Strauch (1996). *Voice and Self: A Handbook of Personal Voice Development Therapy*. London/New York, Free Association Books.

Sundberg, J. (1987). *The Science of the Singing Voice*. Illinois, Northern Illinois University Press.

Tomatis, A. (1991). *The Conscious Ear: My Life of Transformation through Listening*. New York, Station Hill Press.

von Leden, H. (1982). 'A Cultural History of the Human Voice: 1982 Paul Moore Lecture' in *Voice Perspectives*. R. T. Sataloff. London, Singular Publishing Group Inc: 15–86.

Wheatley, M. J. (1999). *Leadership and the New Science*. San Francisco, Berrett-Koehler Publishers.

INDEX

Numbers in italics indicate illustrations.

INDEX

VIKING

UK | USA | Canada | Ireland | Australia
India | New Zealand | South Africa | China

Penguin Books is part of the Penguin Random House group of companies whose addresses can be
found at global.penguinrandomhouse.com.

First published by Penguin Australia Pty Ltd, 2015

Text copyright © Louise Mahler 2015

The moral right of the author has been asserted.

Cover concept Daniel New
Cover and text design by Alissa Dinallo © Penguin Australia Pty Ltd
Internal illustrations by Alissa Dinallo
Author photograph by Jason Smith
Typeset in 12.5/16.5pt Fairfield Light by Alissa Dinallo
Colour separation by Splitting Image Colour Studio, Clayton, Victoria
Printed and bound in Australia by Griffin Press, an accredited ISO AS/NZS 140001 Environmental
Management Systems printer.

National Library of Australia
Cataloguing-in-Publication data:

ISBN: 9780670078905
Mahler, Louise, author.
Resonate: for people who need to be heard / Louise Mahler.
9780670078905 (paperback)
Includes bibliographical references and index.
Oral communication.
Verbal ability.
Communication.
302.224

penguin.com.au